TRANSFIGURATION

New Century Theology

Other books in this series include:

TRANSFIGURATION

Dorothy Lee

New Century Theology

continuum
LONDON • NEW YORK

CONTINUUM
The Tower Building,   15 East 26th Street,
11 York Road,   New York,
London SE1 7NX   NY 10010

www.continuumbooks.com

First published 2004

British Library Cataloguing-in-Publication Data
A catalogue record for this book is available from the British Library.

ISBN 0–8264–7595–7

Typeset by Continuum
Printed and bound by MPG Books Ltd, Bodmin, Cornwall

For Barbara, Ruth, Miriam, Irene, Emma and Jodie

On the mountain, you were transfigured,
and as far as they could
your disciples, Christ our God,
saw your glory;
so that when they saw you crucified,
they might understand you suffered
of your own free will,
and might proclaim to the world
that you are indeed
the Father's reflection.

(from Matins for the Feast of Transfiguration
in Wybrew, 2000, p.111)

Was it a vision?
Or did we see that day the unseeable
One glory of the everlasting world
Perpetually at work, though never seen
Since Eden locked the gate that's everywhere
And nowhere? Was the change in us alone,
And the enormous earth still left forlorn,
An exile or a prisoner? Yet the world
We saw that day made this unreal, for all
Was in its place. The painted animals
Assembled there in gentle congregations,
Or sought apart their leafy oratories,
Or walked in peace, the wild and tame together,
As if, also for them, the day had come.

(from 'The Transfiguration' by Edwin Muir, in Butter, 1991, p.186)

Contents

Foreword

No monograph is ever the work of just one person, despite the solitary name on the cover. A number of people – and communities – have made possible the writing of this book. I thank the Theological Hall and especially the Principal, Peter Matheson, for granting me leave to undertake this study; my colleagues, Christiaan Mostert, Robert Gribben and Brendan Byrne for their theological advice; Grantley McDonald, Miriam Pollard and Peter Blackwood for assisting with details; the Joint Theological Library for locating books and articles; the wonderfully supportive staff of the Theological Hall; my friends at Queen's and Ormond College; Maryanne Confoy and Frank Moloney for ongoing encouragement; the Community of the Transfiguration in Breakwater; and Robin Baird-Smith of Continuum for his patience and support. I am also grateful to Collette Rayment for a conference paper, some years ago, on the transfiguration and the poetry of Peter Steele, which kindled my interest in the subject.

This book, which explores a narrative about six men, is dedicated to six women. In diverse ways, these women have taught me about love, beauty and glory: my mother, my sister, my two daughters and my nieces. Despite his illness and in the midst of his own demanding research, my father, Edwin Lee, found time to listen, suggest and support; to his spirituality I owe the ultimate inspiration for this study. Finally, I thank Maggie who has sat (literally) at my feet for long hours curled into a small, expectant ball of fur, occasionally contributing the odd muddy footprint.

Ormond College
Melbourne
Feast of Saints Cyril and Methodius
14 February 2004

Introduction

The transfiguration tells the story of Jesus' ascent of the mountain some-where at the mid-point of his ministry, in the company of three of his dis-ciples. There his physical appearance is changed, metamorphosing into incandescent light, a light that blazes from his face and clothing. Two of the greatest (long-dead) prophets of Israel's past appear beside him, con-versing with him. The disciples, meanwhile, are overawed at the spectacle and respond with incomprehension and bewilderment, Peter proposing to erect three tents to house Jesus and his celestial guests. At this point a cloud intervenes, overshadowing the heavenly figures, and a voice speaks from the cloud, declaring Jesus to be the beloved Son. Then the miracu-lous signs recede and Jesus is left alone to descend the mountain with his bemused disciples.

With variations, this narrative is told four times in the New Testament, in each of the first three Gospels and in 2 Peter (in abbreviated form), but there are allusions to it elsewhere, particularly the Gospel of John. The story is rich in symbols, with the mountain, the light, and the other images all deriving from Old Testament symbolism and conjuring up a wealth of meaning. In short, the transfiguration provides a powerful evocation of Jesus as the source and bringer of light, who reveals the glory and beauty of God to the disciples. In theological terms, its meaning is inseparably bound up with the incarnation, the cross, the resurrection and the future coming of Christ.

Given its dramatic and theological import, it is strange that the transfiguration should be one of the most neglected stories in the New Testament. This neglect is confined largely to the Western tradition. Christians in the East regard the transfiguration as central to the sym-bolism of the gospel, disclosing as much about themselves as about God. In the West, by contrast, the feast of the transfiguration is a minor event and ignored entirely in some denominational traditions. For the most part, post-Enlightenment biblical scholars have shown little interest in the transfiguration, minimizing its theological status. If anything, biblical studies has tended to 'experience the story as alien' and to 'rationalize this strangeness'.[1]

More recent decades have shown a shift in this perspective and a recovery of a much-neglected but vitally important biblical story. Greater awareness of Eastern Orthodoxy, with its theology and icons, has made a difference. It is no coincidence, moreover, that Pope John Paul II introduced into the saying of the Rosary the 'Luminous Mysteries' – mysteries from the ministry of Jesus as narrated in the Gospels, including the transfiguration.[2] In line with such movements, this book argues for a recovery of the transfiguration story: its theology, symbolism and spirituality. Its neglect may be symptomatic but is more likely causative. Western Christianity in many places is struggling for survival against a deadly secularism that smothers any sense of transcendence or mystery, too much of which has penetrated its own ranks. The Church needs to regain the vision of Christ on the mountain, the light in which we see light, the echo of the divine voice acclaiming Jesus the beloved Son – the biblical symbolism of a majestic, incarnate, crucified God as the only source of hope for the transfiguring of a disfigured world.

To recover the story, we need to recognize that the transfiguration is not an other-worldly narrative, disconnected from the body and ordinary human experience. On the contrary, it is precisely Jesus' transfigured *body* that discloses the face of God and the hope of God's future, addressing the concrete reality of a fearful, uncomprehending group of disciples and a tragic, unbelieving world. In the end, it is as much about their transfiguration, the luminous glory shining in the ordinariness of their flesh, as it is about Jesus' transformation. The transfiguration on the mountain is the meeting-place between human beings and God, between the temporal and the eternal, between past, present and future, between everyday human life – with all its hopes and fears – and the mystery of God. The attachment between them, at every point, is Jesus himself. The transfiguration presents him dressed in the garments of divine light yet clothed also in the garb of creation. He is the point of intersection, the bridge between heaven and earth, the source of hope, bringing to birth – through incarnation, death and resurrection – God's eschatological future.

What kind of narrative is the transfiguration? In general, such questions are important for the reader of any text. The way we read is shaped by the kind of text we think we have before us. Different genres contain different elements; their style and form diverge as well as their modes of expression. For example, the way we read a letter from a friend will be different from the way we read a work of non-fiction. Similarly, we will read a work of non-fiction differently from a novel or short story. As readers we need to know in advance what kind of literature we are reading – even if we have to adjust our ideas along the way. We know before we begin a work of history that the characters exist outside the covers of the book; we know that the characters in a novel (mostly) have no existence outside the author's imagination. Note that the distinction here is not between what is 'real' (history) and 'unreal' (fiction). Historians are also, in a sense, telling a story, one that is also already interpreted; and fiction can represent a profound and truthful exploration of what it means to be human. Sometimes history and fiction seem very close: 'history and literature are equally modes of dealing with, of finding language for, *reality*.'[3] The same is true of the transfiguration – we need to know what kind of literature we are dealing with.

The traditional view (over many centuries) is that the transfiguration story is based on a genuine historical event, even if its meaning is also deeply symbolic; the three disciples are seen as independent eyewitnesses. To the modern scientific mind, however, there are insuperable problems with this view: 'Even on its own terms, the story does not seem plausible.'[4] Peter's ability to recognize Moses and Elijah in a time when Jews did not believe in depicting the human figure is almost inexplicable by contemporary standards. As a result, the presence of Moses and Elijah is seen as a pointer to the importance of the story, rather than something that the Gospel writers expect us to take literally (although Luke may well disagree!). This kind of interpretation reflects the modern tendency to read the story as symbolic rather than historical, though in a limited way.[5] Thus, the emphasis of the story is seen to lie, not on the metamorphosis of Jesus' person, but on the divine voice and what it has to say about Jesus' teaching.[6] Yet here again we encounter problems. Jesus' identity, for the historian, is accessible only in human terms, making the presence of the light and the declaration of Jesus' sonship difficult to classify. Even the category of 'myth' does not assist the modern interpreter, weighed down by the presupposition that mythology (like fairy tales) is somehow not quite real and certainly unrelated to everyday reality.[7]

One way of resolving the problem has been to assume that the transfiguration was originally a resurrection story thrown back into the ministry of Jesus.[8] This interpretation presupposes that the story is out of place in the ministry of Jesus, inconsistent with his more usual conduct. The teaching of Jesus, his suffering and death, even his healing ministry: all these can be made sense of in historical terms, but the transfiguration belongs in a different category entirely. On closer inspection, however, it becomes apparent that the transfiguration is significantly different from the resurrection stories, and thus of a very different genre.[9] Although there are parallels between the transfiguration and the resurrection, these are not numerous or direct enough to warrant regarding the transfiguration as a resurrection story that has lost its way in the maze of Jesus' ministry.

Nevertheless, there are stubborn elements in the transfiguration that suggest an historical kernel, even if we allow for the development of the symbolic. For a story whose chief elements have a cosmic, mythological tone – in the proper sense – the details are surprisingly difficult to interpret. For example, there is no consensus on Peter's suggestion of erecting three tents; it has given rise to a considerable number of explanations, none of which is wholly satisfactory. To interpret the story as a piece of Jewish–Christian invention, based on Moses' ascent of Mount Sinai, is likewise hard to establish, given the allusive nature of the parallels, even in Matthew's account, which are difficult to pin down with any certainty.[10] Taken together with a persistent tradition in mysticism of holy people surrounded by inexplicable light,[11] it is hard to dismiss the transfiguration historically. The symbolism is not as transparent as we might assume had it been the product of Christian imagination. This does not mean that the transfiguration is an ordinary historical event, open to the gaze of the 'neutral' historian.[12] As human beings we lack, as it were, a standpoint from which to view the transfiguration.[13] What a bystander on the mountain may have seen at this extraordinary scene is another question entirely; in the biblical realm, perception depends much on the spiritual capacities of the perceiver.

Even if we cannot dismiss the story too quickly as historical (in some sense), we are still left with the question of genre. There are two possible answers to this question. The first is that the transfiguration is to be read as an apocalyptic vision of the end time, a vision already begun by Jesus in his proclamation of the reign or kingdom of God (Mark 1:14–15).[14] Apocalypticism arose as a movement in Israel in the mid-second century BC in response to intense religious persecution. Its mysterious symbolism was a way of concealing the revelation to all but the insiders, focusing on God's future restoration of Israel and triumph over evil and death. It deals, in other words, with *eschatology*: that is to say, the final advent of God to redeem creation at the end of history. The Old Testament background is located in the apocalyptic visions of Daniel 7–12 which look with hope and expectation to the coming of God's reign, signalled by the heavenly Son of Man (Dan. 7:13). In Mark's Gospel, this hope is already coming into focus in the ministry of Jesus, while retaining its future orientation. In this reading, the transfiguration depicts Jesus as he will be at his future coming, a coming already anticipated in his ministry and resurrection. The focus of the story is on what it reveals of God's glorious future and the central role Jesus plays as God's chosen agent.

The second answer is that the transfiguration is to be read as an epiphany. An epiphany is a literary form which consists of the appearance of a heavenly being on earth with a message for a particular person or group of people.[15] In Luke's Gospel, the annunciation – the appearance of Gabriel to Mary – is such an event (Luke 1:26–38). Old Testament parallels are found in stories such as the visitation of the three angels to Abraham and Sarah at the oaks of Mamre (Gen. 18:1–15), or the appearance of the angel to Balaam which initially only his donkey perceives (Num. 22:22–35).[16] If the transfiguration is indeed an epiphany, it means that it is fundamentally concerned with the revelation of Jesus' heavenly origins and identity, manifest in bodily form in the here-and-now. The emphasis now is on what is revealed of God and God's salvation in the present moment.

It is difficult to choose between these two explanations of the transfiguration. Within the context of New Testament theology, both have their origin in Old Testament understandings of God's relationship with Israel, both are concerned with the relationship between divine and human in the person of Jesus, and both make sense of the transfiguration. We may ask, therefore, why the two interpretations must be seen as mutually exclusive. Is it possible that both genres overlap? If so, the transfiguration can be read as *both* apocalyptic vision and an epiphany. It expresses, on the one hand, the revelation of Jesus' heavenly identity in the context of his ministry and, on the other hand, his role in bringing to birth God's future, where that identity will be fully and finally manifest.

In the following chapters, this book acknowledges that each New Testament version of the transfiguration tells the story in its own way and should not to be assimilated to the other accounts. What is remarkable is that, in so short a tale, there is so much uncertainty and controversy over the details. As often with biblical symbolism, we are attempting as

modern readers to insert ourselves into a world of associations and connotations that we do not inhabit.[17] We begin with the Gospel of Mark,[18] most
probably the earliest of the written Gospels, examining the transfiguration
story in the light of the whole Gospel (Chap 1). Although Mark inherited
the story from oral tradition, it is not our concern to dissect the original
form of the story but to understand it in its Markan context. There follows
a study of Matthew (Chap. 2) then Luke (Chap. 3), both of whom most
probably depended on Mark and edited his story for their own purposes
and in their own ways. Each of these three Gospels – generally called
'Synoptic' because of their close inter-relationship – sets the transfiguration within a wider literary and theological framework. We need, therefore, to take into account the material in each Gospel which parallels, and
thus casts light on, the transfiguration story. From there we move to 2
Peter 1:16–18, which gives a rather different version of the transfiguration
story (Chap. 4).

Finally, we look at transfiguration elements elsewhere in the New
Testament (Chap. 5), especially the Gospel of John, where transfiguration
symbolism seems to permeate its narrative and symbolism. There are
traces of the transfiguration tradition in several Pauline passages and in
the Apocalypse, suggesting a widespread knowledge of the story in the
early Church. Finally, the book concludes with an exploration of the meaning of the transfiguration and its symbolism, drawing together the various
theological strands of the narrative across the New Testament (Chap. 6).

Notes

1 Luz, U., *Matthew 8–20: A Commentary* (trans. J. E. Crouch, ed. H.
  Koester), Fortress, Minneapolis, MN, 2001, 403.
2 The five mysteries are: Jesus' baptism, his self-manifestation at the
  wedding of Cana, his proclamation of the kingdom, the transfiguration, and the institution of the Eucharist.
3 Templeton, D. A., *The New Testament as True Fiction: Literature,
  Literary Criticism, Aesthetics* (ed. G. Aichele), Sheffield Academic
  Press, Sheffield, 1999, 305.
4 Miller, R. D., 'Historicizing the Trans-Historical: The Transfiguration
  Narrative (Mark 9:2–8, Matt. 17:1–8, Luke 9:28–36)', *Forum* 10, 1994,
  246. Miller argues that the transfiguration contains nothing of value
  for reconstructing the life of Jesus (219–48).
5 For an interpretation along these lines, see, e.g., Perry, J. M., *Exploring*

the Transfiguration Story, Sheed & Ward, Kansas City, MO, 1993.

6 The story is often classified as a 'pronouncement story', a narrative whose real import is not the plot itself but rather a climactic saying of, or about, Jesus.

7 For a powerful refutation of this post-Enlightenment view of myth and fairy tale (including their relation to reality), see Tolkien, J. R. R., 'On Fairy Stories', in Tolkien, J. R. R., *Tree and Leaf*, Unwin Books, London, 1964, 43–63.

8 See, e.g., Bultmann, R., *The History of the Synoptic Tradition* (trans. J. Marsh), Blackwell, Oxford, 1963, 259–61. There are also two later apocryphal versions of the transfiguration, in the Ethiopic *Apocalypse of Peter* and the *Pistis Sophia*, which locate it in the resurrection context.

9 See, e.g. Dodd, C. H., 'The Appearances of the Risen Christ: An Essay in Form-Criticism of the Gospels', in Nineham, D. E. (ed.), *Studies in the Gospels: Essays in Memory of R. H. Lightfoot*, Blackwell, Oxford, 1957, 9–35.

10 Both points are raised in Davies, W. D. and Allison, D. C., *A Critical and Exegetical Commentary on the Gospel According to Saint Matthew*, 3 vols (ed. J. A. Emerton et al.), T. & T. Clark, Edinburgh, 1988–97, vol. 2, 692.

11 See Ramsay, M., *The Glory of God and the Transfiguration of Christ*, 2nd edn, Darton, Longman & Todd, London, 1967, 102–3.

12 Discussing the resurrection, O'Collins, G., *The Easter Jesus*, Darton, Longman & Todd, London, 1973, 57–62, draws a distinction between events open to the inspection of the secular historian and events that have their causative origin in God alone.

13 Wink, W., 'Mark 9:2–8', *Interpretation* 36, 1982, 63–4.

14 See, e.g. Kee, H. C., 'The Transfiguration in Mark: Epiphany or Apocalyptic Vision', in Reumann, J. (ed.), *Understanding the Sacred Text: Essays in Honor of Morton S. Enslin on the Hebrew Bible and Christian Beginnings*, Judson Press, Valley Forge, PA, 1972, 135–52. For a survey of theories, see Moses, A. D. A., *Matthew's Transfiguration Story and Jewish–Christian Controversy* (ed. S. E. Porter), Sheffield Academic Press, Sheffield, 1996, 20–6.

15 See Heil, J. P., *The Transfiguration of Jesus: Narrative Meaning and Function of Mark 9:2–8, Matt 17:1–8 and Luke 9:28–36*, Editrice Pontificio Istituto Biblico, Rome, 2000. A disadvantage of this otherwise helpful study is that Heil, op. cit., 37–8, makes too rigid a distinction between

vision (which, he claims, is more subjective), epiphany and theophany.

16 For other Old Testament examples and a fuller discussion, see *ibid.*, 38–73.

17 Nineham, D. E., *Saint Mark*, Penguin Books, Harmondsworth, 1963, 233.

18 The translations offered at the beginning (and occasionally throughout) each chapter – which are my own – are deliberately somewhat rough and inelegant to give the flavour of the original Greek.

1
The Transfiguration in Mark

9:2 And after six days, Jesus took Peter, James and John, and bore them up to a high mountain by themselves in private. And he was transfigured before them, 3 and his clothes became glistening, very white, such as no bleacher on earth could whiten them. 4 And there appeared to them Elijah with Moses and they were talking together with Jesus. 5 Then Peter said to Jesus in response, 'Rabbi, it is good for us to be here; so let us make three tents, one for you, one for Moses and one for Elijah.' 6 For he did not know how to respond, as they were terrified. 7 Then a cloud came overshadowing them, and a voice came out of the cloud: 'This is my beloved Son; listen to him.' 8 And suddenly looking around they no longer saw anyone but Jesus alone with them. 9 And as they were descending the mountain, he instructed them to relate what they had seen to no-one, until the Son of Man should rise from the dead.   (Mark 9:2–9)

Mark tells the story of the transfiguration in simple yet dramatic language. The three phases – ascent, revelation, descent – make use of apocalyptic symbols of light and radiant garments, by which Mark depicts the unfolding drama of God's future, breaking into the grim realities of the present. In this dazzling hope, Jesus' identity as the divine Son is the keystone. In his intimate relationship to God, Jesus is the bearer of the reign (or kingdom) of God, the one through whom God generates that glorious future. The transfiguration story, therefore, speaks as much about Jesus in the present as it does about God's glory in the future; it is as much an epiphany, in the biblical sense, as an apocalyptic drama. The context in which Mark tells his tale makes it clear, moreover, that the glory – which is both an apocalyptic vision and an epiphany – is tied inextricably to suffering and the way of the cross. The poetry of the transfiguration directly addresses the sullen rhetoric of the cross, the beauty of the one turning to embrace the ugliness and squalor of the other.

The transfiguration forms part of Mark's portrayal of the journey to Jerusalem (Mark 8:22–10:52). This journey is structured around three evenly distributed predictions of Jesus' forthcoming passion, death and resurrection. The predictions increase in intensity, the third being the most detailed and comprehensive (8:31; 9:31–2; 10:32–4). They form the backbone to Jesus' teaching in this section of the Gospel, while the journey itself is symbolic, concerned to reveal Jesus' identity and his destiny in Jerusalem, as well as what it means to follow Jesus as a disciple. Mark sees discipleship as flowing from Christology – that is, from his understanding of Jesus – so that the revealing of Jesus' identity is bound up with the calling of disciples.[1] Following each prediction along the way to Jerusalem, Mark exposes the misunderstanding of the disciples (8:32–3; 9:33–7; 10:35–45), a misunderstanding that will climax in their betrayal, flight and denial in the passion narrative. The journey is framed by two stories of blind men receiving their sight, one at the beginning and one at the end (8:22–6; 10:46–52).

Standing at the commencement of the journey to Jerusalem, the transfiguration story thus occupies a strategic position in Mark's Gospel. Indeed, it is part of a diptych that stands at the heart of the Markan narrative, two central panels at the mid-point of the Gospel (8:27–9:13).[2] In the first panel (8:31–8), Jesus at Caesarea Philippi predicts his death and resurrection, unfolding his identity as the suffering, dying, rising and returning Son of Man to his astounded disciples. He speaks of the way of the cross as implying a life of renunciation, self-denial, and voluntary powerlessness. In the second panel, where Jesus is transfigured on the mountain before his frightened and uncomprehending disciples, his identity is again revealed, in different though complementary terms. On either side of the two central scenes, Jesus and his disciples discuss his identity in relation to John the Baptist and Elijah. In the second of these, the first passion and resurrection prediction at 8:31 is confirmed.

In the centre of the sequence, between the two panels, is a transitional saying introduced by 'I tell you solemnly' (9:1). This rather puzzling saying leads from one panel to the other, bringing the first scene to a climax and setting the second scene in motion.[3] The promise of the Son of Man's future glorious return, says Jesus, will even now be fulfilled in the lifetime of some of those present. While this probably refers to the promise of the risen Christ's presence with his disciples, its more immediate meaning must be the transfiguration. What the revelation at the centre of Mark's Gospel is about is the reign of God (*basileia*: 1:15; 4:11; 11:10; 14:62), a coming that is dependent on Jesus' identity and divinely-given destiny. The revelation is directed at those disciples who will 'see' in their lifetime

God's future reign, breaking into the present with transforming power. Note that at the empty tomb the young man in white will tell the disciples that it is in Galilee they will 'see him' (16:7). The symbolism of seeing is thus important for Mark, especially on a journey bound by two blind men who receive sight, in contrast to the disciples who fail to see.[4] To see means more than the visual sight of Jesus: it is a discerning seeing that arises from faith.

The theme of the Markan diptych is primarily Jesus' identity, which is both manifest and secret at the same time. Throughout, there is a procession of voices that addresses the question of Jesus' identity, each moving closer to the innermost circle: other people (8:27), the disciples ('you', 8:29), Jesus himself ('the Son of Man', 8:31, 39), and finally the voice of God from the cloud (9:7).[5] At the same time, linked to the question of identity is the motif of faith and discipleship flowing from Mark's understanding of Jesus. The whole unit may be illustrated as shown in Table 1.1.

Table 1.1

Introduction	PANEL 1: SUFFERING (villages of C.P.)	→Transition	PANEL 2: GLORY (mountain)	Conclusion
• Secrecy of revelation • Role of Elijah and John the Baptist • Disciples' lack of understanding (8:27–30)	Revelation of Jesus to disciples as suffering Son of Man, who will rise from the dead and return in glory (8:31–8)	Seeing God's reign come in power (9:1)	Revelation of Jesus to three disciples as beloved Son, transfigured in radiance and light (9:2–9)	• Secrecy of revelation • Role of Elijah and John the Baptist • Disciples' lack of understanding (9:10–13)

Because modern biblical scholars tend to play down the transfiguration, they often underestimate the importance of the second scene, highlighting instead the first with its message of suffering – the way of the cross that commences at the height of Jesus' Galilean ministry. As a result, the transfiguration becomes little more than a footnote in the revelation of the cross. Mark is venerated as the martyrs' Gospel, the Gospel of the suffering Son of Man, with its sympathetic portrayal of Jesus' human struggle to carry out the dark, divine will. Suffering is certainly integral to Mark's theological message, and the divine voice at the transfiguration does instruct the disciples to listen to Jesus as he teaches, and walks, the sorrowful path. But the necessity of Jesus' suffering cannot be isolated from the revelation on the mountain. The two panels – passion prediction on the road to Caesarea Philippi and Jesus as the Son on the mountain – belong together, each incomplete without the other. Suffering *and* glory stand together at the heart of Mark's Gospel. Indeed, both dimensions are in one sense present in each of the two scenes. Resurrection, future coming and glory are explicitly referred to in the first scene (8:31, 38), while suffering is implied by the command to listen to Jesus in the second (9:7). In either event, both themes challenge the disciples' expectations of the coming Messiah. Both direct the disciples to God's reign, as it unfolds on the road and on the mountain.

The transfiguration story itself has a simple structure, framed by Jesus' ascent and descent of the mountain in company with his three disciples; in the middle is the transfiguration itself and its attendant heavenly signs, with Peter's response as the centre (Table 1.2).

Table 1.2

---

a Setting:
Jesus ascends mountain
with three disciples (9:2a)

         b Revelation of Heavenly
         Signs:
         • Jesus transfigured
         • Moses and Elijah (9:2b–4)

                        c Disciples' Response:
                        Peter, tents, confusion,
                        fear (9:5–6)

         b¹ Revelation and
         Interpretation of Signs:
         • the cloud
         • the voice (9:7)

a¹ Conclusion:
Jesus descends mountain
with disciples (9:8–9)

This structure, technically called a 'chiasm' – for its *a b b a* pattern – makes plain the important role played by the disciples as witnesses to the transfiguration. They are present both in the frame (**a** and **a¹**) and at the centre (**c**) of the story. Yet, as we shall see, the revelation of Jesus and its heavenly interpretation form the narrative backbone (**b** and **b¹**), to which the disciples respond. Their role is to testify to the transfiguration after the resurrection, when the revelation in Jesus will be complete (9:9). Peter's response enacts the misunderstanding of the disciples as a whole, though it is not without insight.

Mark's transfiguration story begins with an unusual time reference: 'six days later' (9:2a). This is strange given that Mark is not usually specific about time outside the passion story. It is possible that the six days reference has a symbolic function. It could be a time-marker, for example, that sees the seventh day as the day of climax following the revelation at Caesarea Philippi.[6] Or there may be a parallel with Moses on Mount Sinai (Exod. 24).[7] There the cloud settles on the mountain for six days before Moses ascends to receive the two tablets of the law (Exod. 24:16), written 'with the finger of God' (Exod. 31:18). The Sinai parallel is not an exact fit but an allusion that does not cancel out other possibilities. What is patent is the connection between the transfiguration and the saying at 9:1.

This is not the only occasion in Mark's Gospel where the three disciples are singled out by Jesus. Peter, James and John are among the first four to be called by Jesus (1:16–20). All three, along with Andrew, are present at the healing of Peter's mother-in-law (1:29–31). They participate in Jesus' lifestyle and ministry, coming under fire from the religious authorities (2:16, 23–4; 7:1–16). They are among the twelve appointed to 'be with him', sent out to proclaim and cast out demons (3:14–15). Their names appear at the head of the list and they are the only ones to be given nicknames: 'Peter' meaning 'rock' (though, since it is Greek, Mark does not explain it) and 'Boanerges' meaning 'sons of thunder' (3:16–17). Belonging to the circle of Jesus' new family, they are given the key to the mystery of God's reign (4:11, 34). Along with the other disciples, they witness Jesus' mighty acts and are awestruck by the one whom 'even the winds and sea obey' (4:41). The same three witness Jairus' twelve-year-old daughter rise from the dead (5:40–2). They are among those sent out on the mission (6:7–13), returning with a sense of achievement (6:30). Yet already the twelve show signs of failing to grasp the mystery of God's reign, for all their willingness to follow. After the dual feeding episodes, Jesus exposes their hardness of heart (8:14–21). It is not surprising that, as this mystery deepens with the revelation of Jesus' suffering and glory, the disciples' incomprehension likewise deepens. Peter's confession at

Caesarea Philippi receives not commendation (as in Matthew's Gospel), but a stern command to secrecy, and Peter's subsequent reaction to the first passion and resurrection prediction confirms the limited nature of his understanding (8:29–33).[8]

Here for the second, though not last, time in the Gospel, Jesus takes the three disciples aside – privileged, self-sacrificing yet also stubborn and uncomprehending – leading them up the high mountain for the second stage of his self-revelation (see 13:1–37; 14:32–42). Already Jesus has alluded at 9:1 to the fact that some of those present will not die until 'the reign of God has come in power'. For the evangelist, at this moment, Peter, James and John represent those 'standing here' who will gain a vision of God's transforming reign. Indeed, everything in the story points intentionally to the disciples: Jesus 'bears *them* up' (literally) to the mountain, he is transfigured *before them* (9:2), Elijah and Moses appear *to them* (9:4), Peter's suggestion is described as his *response* to these events (9:5), the voice coming *out of* the cloud addresses the disciples, and as they descend the mountain Jesus enjoins secrecy (9:9), a secrecy they are to unveil at the proper time.[9] Mark tells the story from the vantage-point of the disciples.

Other symbols of the transfiguration have a similar wealth of meaning. One of the richest is that of the mountain. In ancient cosmology, a high mountain stands on the boundary between heaven and earth. In the Graeco-Roman pantheon, for example, people thought that the gods dwelt on the heights of Mount Olympus under the command of Zeus/Jupiter, king of gods and mortals. Judaism too shared a somewhat similar cosmology, though not in so literal a way. The Old Testament identifies several mountains as the 'mountain of God' and associates them with revelation,[10] the most famous being Mount Sinai which Moses ascends to receive the gift of the law, entering into the glorious presence of God. Prior to that, the revelation of the divine name and God's commissioning of Moses at the burning bush occur on Mount Horeb (Exodus 3).[11] Like Moses, Elijah too experiences a vision of God on Mount Horeb: not in the noisy wind or earthquake or fire but paradoxically in a 'sound of sheer silence' (1 Kgs 19:11–13).

Mount Sion is also important symbolically, even though it is a different location to Horeb/Sinai. The symbolism, however, coheres. The holy city of Jerusalem, on the top of the mountain, is the city of God, the habitation God loves above any other (Ps. 87:1–2). The temple especially is the place where God's glory dwells (e.g. Ps. 25:8; Wis. 9:8), where God is to be seen in awesome holiness and beauty (Isa. 6:1–4). In other places, the mountain of God – associated with Sion – is eschatological: it depicts the glory of the last days when righteousness and peace will flourish, symbolized in the final banquet (see Isa. 11:6–9; 25:6–10a). From the sanctuary of the temple, streams of living water will flow for growth and healing (Ezek. 47:1–12). The mountain of God in the Old Testament is thus a numinous place where the air, in more senses than one, is thin: revelation, the law, epiphany, divine indwelling, the end time.

Mark gives no indication of the actual mountain on which the transfiguration takes place. Origen (185–254 AD) and Cyril of Jerusalem (*c.* 315–86 AD) identified the site as Mount Tabor, a tradition that persists today. Tabor is not impossible as a location, although it is not strictly a high mountain (1350 ft), lies some distance from Caesarea Philippi (south of Capernaum), and in the first century AD had a Roman fortification on its summit. Other possibilities include Mount Hermon, which is much higher (9200 ft) and just north of Caesarea Philippi – being the source of the Jordan – and also Mount Meron (3926 ft) in Upper Galilee. Nevertheless, the actual venue is unimportant for Mark. What matters is that Jesus stands, as Moses and Elijah before him, on the mountain of God, at the boundary between heaven and earth, 'on the outskirts of heaven'.[12] Unlike the baptism, which has strong parallels with the transfiguration, nothing is said of the heavens opening, since 'the mountain-top setting obviates a sky-opening'.[13] Indeed, Jesus himself represents the bridge between heaven and earth, as the divine voice testifies (9:7; also at the baptism, 1:10–11). In one sense, therefore, we can speak of the mountain as a symbol of Jesus himself, with the geography – as elsewhere in this Gospel – serving as a symbol for Mark's Christology.

The most spectacular symbol of the transfiguration is the change in Jesus' clothing, which becomes radiantly white, beyond anything in the natural realm (9:2b–3). The transformation (*metemorphôthê*) is miraculous, unearthly, 'such as no bleacher on earth could whiten them'.[14] Mark is not speaking literally of white but rather the 'colour' of light, a light that transcends the natural world. It is a divine hue, showing Jesus' true identity, an identity hidden from human eyes thus far in the Gospel – though implied in everything Jesus says and does – but now triumphantly released to the disciples on the mountain. This is the same numinous clothing from which healing power has come earlier in the Gospel (5:27–32; 6:56),[15] the clothing over which the soldiers will cast lots at the crucifixion (15:20, 24).

White clothing is particularly characteristic of heavenly beings in the apocalyptic writings of Judaism and early Christianity. Apocalyptic theology is concerned with eschatology, the advent of God's future reign on earth. In this literature, God's appearance is associated with whiteness, light and fire, all three elements being closely linked. In the vision of Daniel that Mark quotes elsewhere in his Gospel, the Ancient One is garbed in garments 'white as snow', a stream of fire issuing from his presence (13:26; Dan. 7:9; 1 Enoch 14:20). Similarly, the angelic beings who stand in the presence of God are clothed in radiant white garments (16:5; 2 Macc. 11:8). By extension, the righteous in heaven will also be clothed in white, wearing celestial garb as befits their status and abode (e.g. 1 Enoch 62:15; 2 Enoch 22:8–10; 4 Ezra 2:39; Apoc. 3:5; 6:11; 7:9, 13–14; 19:14). Yet it is strange, given these associations, that only Jesus' clothing is described as white and radiant. Mark does not extend the same description to Moses and Elijah; indeed nothing is said of their raiment or demeanour. The portrayal of Jesus' radiance suggests that his identity, like his physical appearance, is unique.

Mark makes no explicit mention of Jesus' face being changed, unlike Matthew and Luke (Matt. 17:2; Luke 9:29). Yet Mark's actual wording is ambiguous. He describes the change in Jesus' appearance in two statements: Jesus was transfigured *and* his clothes become dazzlingly white. This could mean that the whiteness of his clothing was the medium of the transfiguration, the word 'and' being explanatory: 'he was transfigured before them in that his clothes became white.' Alternatively, it could be an inclusive statement: 'he was transfigured before them, including his clothes'. In this case, the change in Jesus' clothing – which 'only confirms the unearthly character of his appearance'[16] – would extend to his whole physical form.[17] If so, the reference to the transfigured clothing in Mark is a form of metonymy, a figure of speech where the part stands for the whole. It is possible, therefore, that even for Mark Jesus' entire body is metamorphosed: 'Jesus is transfigured, not merely His clothes.'[18]

Mark implies that Jesus' transfiguration is the revelation of his glory (*doxa*), although the actual word does not appear in the story itself. Yet the previous scene has already spoken of the Son of Man's future return in glory (8:38), a glory that the transfiguration seems to anticipate. Mark is again drawing on apocalyptic traditions – which display the hope of God's future triumph – as well as employing symbolism associated with Sion in the Old Testament. The two traditions flow together: glory refers back to the indwelling of God on Mount Sion in the temple, on the one hand, and forwards to the final fulfilment of God's reign, on the other. Jesus' whole being on the mountain is suffused with the saving presence of God;[19] surrounded by the glory of the *Shekinah*, the divine presence redolent with indwelling light.[20]

But do the light and glory of the transfiguration come from within Jesus himself, as the expression of his hidden self, or are they the gift of God coming from without? The divine voice speaking out of the cloud suggests the latter: that it comes from beyond Jesus and depicts 'Jesus' entrance into the Shekinah ... Jesus' unique envelopment in the heart of God'.[21] Yet the light shines only from Jesus himself, and from no other, intimating that the metamorphosis is also, paradoxically, the outward manifesting of Jesus' identity, an identity that is nonetheless dependent upon God. In either case, the light that Jesus displays illuminates his whole being, extending even to his clothing, and will be vindicated at his final coming, his parousia.[22] The symbolism indicates that Jesus belongs not just in the earthly world but also the heavenly; not just in the present but also God's future. The glory has its source in God but it is also a glory that Jesus himself possesses from his first appearance in Mark's Gospel (1:9–11) – a glory given, not borrowed, interiorized, forming a unique selfhood that, while bestowed by God, belongs also to Jesus. His radiance is at once the dramatic symbol of his inimitable relationship to the heavenly realm – his unique favour with God – and his own interiority and self-awareness.

In a similar way, the symbolism of Moses and Elijah as Jesus' celestial companions indicates something of Jesus' identity (9:4). The reversed chronological placement in which Mark introduces them at first seems strange: 'Elijah with Moses'. The clue to the word order is probably found once again in the realm of apocalyptic symbolism. There were expectations in Judaism that Elijah would appear at the end time as the messenger of God's reign. Malachi speaks of Elijah as the eschatological prophet who will come 'before the great and terrible day of the Lord' (Mal. 4:5). At the beginning of Mark's Gospel, a verse from Malachi precedes the quote from Isaiah which introduces John the Baptist, setting the prophecy in the light of God's future: 'Behold I send my messenger before your face' (1:2–3). Similarly at the transfiguration the priority of Elijah ensures an eschatological orientation to the Markan narrative – we now know that Mark here is concerned with God's final advent.[23] Mark makes a good deal of Elijah and sees John the Baptist, in one sense, as the fulfilment of Malachi's promise; Mark's Jesus likewise shares the fate of Elijah/John the Baptist,

who are subjected to persecution and rejection. So too at the transfiguration, the prominence given to Elijah coheres with Mark's theological
concerns. Because Mark sees Elijah as an end-time figure, and because
Elijah has influenced his portrayal of both John the Baptist and
Jesus, Elijah's name precedes Moses as the more important figure in this
context.

The traditional reading that Moses and Elijah represent the law and
the prophets has its problems. In the Old Testament, Moses is not just the
giver of the law but also the greatest of the prophets. Judaism had expectations of a 'prophet-like-Moses' who would arise to speak the word of the
Lord in a way that the people of God would hear (Deut. 18:15–18). In a
parallel way, the prophet Elijah (whose name is associated with no actual
prophetic writings) is a champion of the law over against idolatry. In fact,
Elijah himself does not die but is assumed into heaven in a fiery chariot (2
Kgs 2:1–12). The Book of Deuteronomy makes reference to Moses' death
and burial (Deut. 34:5–6), but the circumstances are mysterious and the
site of the grave unknown. The mystery surrounding his burial gave rise
to speculation, in some Jewish circles, that Moses too, like Elijah and
Enoch (Gen. 5:21–4), had perhaps never actually 'tasted death',[24] but had
been assumed into heaven.[25] Both Moses and Elijah are thus major
prophets of Israel's past, associated in some way with bypassing death.
Both receive epiphanies on Horeb/Sinai that shape the future of Israel
(Exodus 3; 24; 34; 1 Kgs 19:1–11). Both in different ways, even in their
frailties, exemplify fidelity and obedience to God.

There is also a mystical dimension to the presence of Elijah and Moses.
They represent what Christians later came to call the 'communion of
saints' – the heavenly world with which Jesus is in communion. In this
sense their significance is more subjective: they inhabit not only the celestial realm but also Jesus' own spiritual world.[26] Their external manifestation mirrors their internal presence within Jesus himself, indicating their
importance for his spirituality. Although Mark (unlike Luke) says nothing
of the subject of conversation between the three exalted figures on the
mountain, the very fact that they are portrayed as 'speaking together'
emphasizes their union and communion. While the transfiguration is narrated from the viewpoint and for the sake of the disciples, it would be a
mistake to lose sight of what Jesus himself experiences. His transfiguration is bound up in his awareness of these two giants of Old Testament history and spirituality – prophets who knew God intimately and who shaped
the destiny of Israel with their faith and insight.

Moses and Elijah are thus complex symbols, representing God's ancient people, Israel, and associated with mountain epiphanies and the events of the end time. One thing is clear in the range of possible meanings. For Mark, the symbolic significance is unmistakably Christological: their presence acts as a dual pointer to the identity of Jesus himself. It is no coincidence that they appear at the very moment of Jesus' metamorphosis, opening up past, present and future to the heavenly world, and giving a cosmic perspective on the human world embodied in Israel. As his celestial attendants,[27] Moses and Elijah point symbolically to Jesus, standing 'in the role of Jesus' sponsors'.[28] They remain long enough to present him as the fulfilment of all they stand for in Israel's past and election by God. Like the unearthly white of Jesus' garments, Moses and Elijah, even while not partaking of his brightness, disclose Jesus' heavenly identity, an identity superior to them in every way. With both continuity and vivid contrast, therefore, God 'brought forth the leading prophets so that [the disciples] could see how great a difference there was between slaves and the Master'.[29]

Standing at the centre of the narrative is Peter's response to the symbols of transfiguration (9:5–6). Mark illustrates Peter's enthusiasm but also his woeful lack of comprehension. Indeed, the suggestion that three tents be constructed to house Jesus and his guests is surprisingly difficult to make sense of and Mark has to explain in an editorial aside that Peter's request shows his (and the other disciples') misunderstanding as a result of fear (9:6). Whatever Peter actually intends by his spontaneous outburst, either Mark himself can make no sense of it or Peter's associations are comprehensible, albeit incorrect. Both options would explain Mark's editorial comment. If Peter has a specific meaning and is not just babbling incoherently from fear,[30] we should be able to pin down his assumptions.[31] There are three possible meanings. The first is that the transfiguration recalls to Peter's mind the Jewish feast of Tabernacles. Originally a harvest festival, Tabernacles required that worshippers live for the duration in tents or huts, constructed from leaves and branches, as a reminder of their wandering in the wilderness. Later the feast acquired eschatological significance, looking joyfully to God's redemption at the end time (Lev. 23:33–6; Deut. 16:13–15).[32] If this background fits the Markan context, then Peter's mistake would be his assumption that the last days have already come. Yet the problem with this view is why Peter would not propose the construction of six tents rather than three. Surely the disciples would see themselves as participants in such an event, just as they would expect to participate in the festivities of Tabernacles?

The second possibility is that Peter is reminded of the tent of meeting in the wilderness, where long ago God spoke to Moses outside the camp of the Israelites (Exod. 33:7–11; Deut. 31:14–15). This interpretation would mean that, in Peter's eyes, the transfiguration – and especially the communion between Jesus, Moses and Elijah – signifies the re-opening of an ancient channel of communication, a channel requiring an earthly edifice. Yet why, in that case, would Peter propose three tents instead of one? During the wilderness period, there was only ever one tent for Moses to commune with God. Peter would hardly suggest the erecting of three tents where only one is required by the Old Testament symbolism.

The third possibility has its source in more overtly apocalyptic texts which, as we have already seen, have had a powerful influence on Mark's theology. Peter may well be thinking of the eternal tents in which the righteous will dwell with the angels at the end time (1 Enoch 39:3–8; Testament of Abraham A 20:13–14).[33] This context would certainly cohere with the fact that Jesus is wearing the proper attire, clad in the garments of heaven. Peter's mistake would then lie in equating Moses and Elijah with Jesus, placing all three on the same level, as if there were no difference between them. If so, his mistake is quickly countered by the divine voice from the cloud, which singles out Jesus alone, and by the sudden disappearance of Moses and Elijah. This third explanation makes some sense, but it too is not without problems. Why is nothing said of Moses and Elijah's raiment, if such be the case? And why should Peter think such flimsy constructions would achieve his aim of providing permanent abodes for the three 'holy ones'?

The simplest and most popular explanation is that Peter wants to hold onto the experience and prolong the glory in any way he can, including the marvellous presence of Moses and Elijah. Understandably, he does not want this terrifying yet exhilarating moment to end. In this view, Peter fails to appreciate the future eschatological significance of what is revealed on the mountain and the necessity of Jesus' intervening suffering and death. As in the previous scene – with which the transfiguration is so closely bound – it becomes clear that Peter still wants Jesus to bypass the cross (8:32). This view is attractive as far as it goes, particularly if we detect a mistaken kind of eschatology in Peter's desires: his assumption that the end time has already come. However, this interpretation explains *that* but not *how* he misunderstands. No more than previous options does it demonstrate precisely how three temporary shelters can achieve the permanence Peter has in mind.

It is not easy to choose between these interpretations; all have possibilities and all have problems. It is most likely that we are in no position to tell exactly what Peter does intend.[34] Mark makes no effort to explain specifically what Peter's words denote and our attempts to pinpoint his meaning may, in fact, take us beyond the scope of the text. If this is right, a number of biblical and symbolic associations will naturally occur to the well-read reader – the feast of Tabernacles, the tent of meeting, the eternal dwellings of the righteous – but none can be pinned down with any certainty. We are left puzzled by Peter's 'uncertain and confused offer',[35] a puzzle that Mark himself does not attempt to resolve. Indeed, it may be that Peter himself is unclear of his precise meaning, his words being a spontaneous outburst provoked by the confusing emotions that the transfiguration evokes. Thus, while the three tents may well have symbolic value in Mark's tale, they are clearly an inadequate symbol, either inept or positively misleading. Peter's words reveal his misunderstanding when confronted by the glorious mystery of God's reign and the path that it takes to attain fulfilment.

At the same time, it would be a mistake to conclude that Peter is entirely wrong in his impulses. Along with his misunderstanding is joy at being present at such an event. His fear at its unexpected majesty and glory may, in any case, be closer to awe than mere fright,[36] although it is not easy to separate the two, especially in Mark's Gospel. Peter is right on both counts, even if Mark's language seems understated. Joy and fear are the normal human emotions to an epiphany and, at one level, entirely appropriate. Peter's immediate reaction, that 'it is good that we are here',[37] is also fitting; after all, Jesus has brought him up the mountain for precisely this purpose. The fact that the three disciples cannot grasp the experience and so misunderstand it does not detract from what they have genuinely seen and perceived. The change in Jesus' body and the appearance of Moses and Elijah are indeed uniquely 'good' (*kalon*), just as it is 'good' for the three disciples to behold the beauty unveiled before them.[38] Confronted by these two extraordinary figures of the past, and in company with a radically altered yet still recognizable Jesus, Peter rightly 'recognizes their indissoluble connection with Christ'.[39] For this reason, Peter's use of the title 'Rabbi' is surprisingly minimal in this context (though changed by both Matthew and Luke), especially given his faith-confession of the week before (8:29). Perhaps Peter is stammering, too overcome by what is happening to know what he is saying. Overall, his response betrays a mixture of insight, misunderstanding and awe.[40]

Peter's response is followed, almost at once, by the intervention of the overshadowing cloud and the words of the divine voice: 'This is my beloved Son; listen to him' (9:7). While being symbolic in themselves, these also help to elucidate the symbolic meaning of what has already taken place. Inasmuch as Peter is placing the three heavenly beings on an equal footing, the voice functions as a corrective to Peter's misapprehension (although Jesus at least has priority on his list): 'Peter wanted three tabernacles but the heavenly response showed him that we have but one.'[41] Yet the cloud and the voice are more than correctives; they are integral to the transfiguration. The voice from the cloud reveals the hidden, divine presence behind this event, the origin and goal of all that happens. It also functions as an interpretation of what has happened to Jesus, both in his bodily transposition and the appearance of his heavenly attendants.[42] In each case, we are told, these are the tangible symbols indicating his identity as the beloved Son.

The cloud itself is not a natural phenomenon, any more than the light, despite the common occurrence of cloud on high mountain peaks. Its sudden appearance is miraculous and seems to embrace only the three heavenly figures.[43] The verb 'overshadow' in the Greek Old Testament means literally 'to cast a shade', with the sense of covering or even sheltering (*episkiazein*).[44] This suggests that the cloud actually conceals Jesus, Moses and Elijah from the gaze of the disciples.[45] The fact that the voice comes 'out of the cloud' (9:7) likewise suggests that the disciples are outside, their role as onlookers being to bear witness to both cloud and voice. In the Old Testament, and particularly the wilderness tradition, the cloud is associated with the guiding hand of God and the *Shekinah*: the 'pillar of cloud' that leads the children of Israel through the wilderness by day, in addition to the 'pillar of fire' by night (Exod. 13:21–2; 40:36–8). The same cloud hovers over the tent of the covenant (Num. 9:15–17) and over the mercy seat (Lev. 16:2), and is associated with the glory of the Lord (Exod. 16:10). Mount Sinai is shrouded in cloud when Moses ascends to receive the law (Exod. 24:15–18; 34:5). In each case, the cloud is a symbol of God's saving presence, God's gracious self-manifestation to, and protection of, Israel through exodus and liberation. The cloud thus signals divine presence and divine revelation; it is a 'better tabernacle' than the three suggested by Peter.[46]

Nevertheless, the Markan narrative at first reading suggests the very opposite: that the cloud conceals rather than reveals, covers rather than uncovers.[47] Although this assumption seems to go against the symbolism of Exodus and Sinai where the cloud discloses the reassuring presence of God, the opposite is also true. Even in the Old Testament the cloud as symbol of divine presence conveys a sense of unutterable holiness that stands over against the creaturely world. In Exodus 24, for example, only Moses is permitted to enter the cloud. God's presence thus retains the quality of mystery even in its most profound self-disclosure. That which conceals also reveals. The more that is revealed of God's self-giving in Mark's Gospel (as in the Sinai tradition), the more mysterious, incomprehensible and awesome that divine revelation appears. The cloud signifies 'the visible form of the governing, guiding and yet hidden form of Yahweh's presence'.[48] Mark confronts the disciples with an identity that is both revealed and concealed at the same time: covered over by their inability to comprehend but even more fundamentally by the very mystery of who and what God is, a God who is made known yet remains elusive (see 4:41). Perhaps there is also a sense of the shadowy cloud protecting the three disciples from a sight too awesome for them to contemplate.

It is important at this point to underline that the story of the transfiguration is not just about the word of God. Some have argued that the climax of the transfiguration is the divine voice, with its proclamation of Jesus' identity and confirmation of his teaching.[49] The structure of the story suggests, on the contrary, that the identity of Jesus is revealed first and foremost in his metamorphosis: on their descent of the mountain Jesus forbids the disciples to report 'what they had *seen*' (9:9). The voice from the cloud functions to interpret the significance of the heavenly portents, making clear that what is taking place is the unveiling of Jesus' mysterious identity as the divine Son. The actual transfiguration of Jesus is not a peripheral detail, a setting of the scene, but rather the purpose of the entire episode. His bodily appearance changes because his true identity, hidden from the eyes of the world, is unveiled to the astonished gaze of the disciples. The transfiguration, therefore, does not just vindicate Jesus' teaching on the way of the cross. More fundamentally, it is concerned to unveil the source and certainty of salvation.[50] The divine voice proclaiming Jesus' identity to the disciples as 'the beloved Son' is an interpretative voice, further unfolding the meaning of the transfiguration.

It is true that the title 'son of God' (*huios tou theou*), understood in its precise Old Testament background, is not of itself a title for the Messiah; nor is it essentially divine. An important background text is Psalm 2:7, a royal psalm in which God addresses the newly-crowned king as son, 'begotten' of God, language that is used in a strictly metaphorical sense.[51]

In Mark's hands, however, the title gains a more exalted connotation in the light of Jesus' unique relationship to God.[52] It is critically placed within the Markan Gospel, moreover, giving it a context that implies more than the royal associations of the Old Testament. 'Son of God' appears in the heading of the Gospel: 'The beginning of the good news of Jesus Christ, Son of God' (1:1).[53] The divine voice at Jesus' baptism addresses him directly as 'my beloved Son' (1:11). The Gerasene demoniac, under the influence of multiple demons (who, while being evil, nonetheless inhabit the same cosmic realm), cries out: 'What have I to do with you, Jesus, Son of the most high God?' (5:7). In addition to the transfiguration, Jesus on trial admits to the horrified high priest his unique identity as 'the Christ, the Son of the Blessed One' (14:61). Finally, the title 'Son of God' is found on the lips of the Roman centurion immediately after Jesus' death (15:39).

Jesus' sonship, in other words, is 'linked with key moments in the life of Jesus',[54] including his transfiguration. It signifies his royal status within the coming-yet-present reign of God. It expresses his filial obedience to God as his sovereign Father who, for Jesus, is utterly trustworthy, even if that trust is still to be vindicated in the future.[55] It also includes, alongside the royalty and sovereignty, a profound sense of intimacy: as God's uniquely beloved, Jesus addresses him as *'abba'* and 'my God' (14:35; 15:34).[56] Mark's use of 'Son' thus outlines an identity that cannot be encapsulated even within Old Testament categories,[57] and suggests an identity that transcends any human framework. In this sense, Jesus' sonship is unique rather than representative.[58] The voice from the cloud confirms Jesus' status as both royal and divine:[59] 'In Markan Christology ... there can be no dichotomy between a royal interpretation of Jesus' divine sonship and a concept of that sonship that sees Jesus as participating in some way in God's very power and being.'[60] The Gospel which presents the most human side to Jesus – his suffering, struggle and anguish – also emphasizes his radiance and authority as Son, an authority that no other possesses, not even such superlative prophets as Moses and Elijah.[61]

Jesus' identity as the beloved Son is the basis on which the divine voice adjures the disciples to 'listen to him'. This instruction makes particular sense of the journey to Jerusalem where Jesus will teach the reluctant disciples the significance of the way of the cross. It reinforces the passion and resurrection predictions, validating the 'economy of the cross',[62] and communicating to the reader that the path Jesus takes is the path of divine necessity, undertaken by the Son in obedience to the Father. Yet the injunction is more than that. In Moses' farewell speech, as we have already noted, the people are promised a prophet like Moses, who will be the voice of God and to whom Israel will listen (Deut. 18:15–18). Just as Moses is the mouth of God in the old covenant, therefore, so Jesus is the mouth of God in the new. Yet Jesus is more than a prophet in Mark's narrative; the disciples are not instructed to give heed to Moses but to Jesus. As the Son of the Father, his association with the divine voice is much closer – so much so that everything he speaks is directly from the mouth of God. To hear Jesus' words is to hear the divine voice. The proximity of the cloud to Jesus, as well as the divine speech that issues from it, makes that point clear. The word of God is radically identified with the teaching of Jesus; like God's word in the Old Testament, it is utterly effective and consequential. Until then, they will remain silent, as Jesus instructs (9:9). As the divine Son, Jesus at the transfiguration embodies the mouth, the word, the speech and thus the deeds, of God's own self.

With this beloved Son, who is the voice of God, the three disciples are finally left alone and at once begin their descent down the mountain (9:8). The sensory signs are gone from sight and hearing: the light, the cloud, the voice, the presence of Moses and Elijah. All is as it was on their arrival – Jesus has resumed his familiar form and appearance. There is something startling, however, about the way Mark describes the sudden disappearance of the heavenly symbols, as if the disciples stare for a moment, rubbing their eyes, as bemused by the vanishing as by their sudden appearance. The conversation that follows does little to enlighten them (9:9–11). Although they may not yet realize it, they are now armed for the approaching journey and its disturbing end by the sight of the vision and the hearing of the voice. Nor will they comprehend until the tale is told: when the Shepherd, having been struck, rises again to re-gather his scattered sheep (14:27–8).

The transfiguration not only holds a critical place in the centre of the Gospel and at the beginning of the journey to Jerusalem, it also shares characteristics with other episodes at the beginning and end of the Gospel. The first of these is the baptism of Jesus by John the Baptist, a puzzling account which Mark narrates in the briefest and baldest of terms (1:9–11). At first glance Jesus is simply one of a large crowd coming from everywhere to be baptized in the Jordan river 'while confessing their sins' (1:5). Yet almost at once this impression is revised. In place of the confession of sins, Jesus ascends from the water and sees the heavens open and the Spirit descending on him like a dove (1:10). The divine voice speaks out, boldly acclaiming him: 'you are my beloved Son, in whom I am well pleased' (1:11). The voice at the baptism is the same voice that speaks at the transfiguration, in similar wording, but addressed only to Jesus. What we have in the transfiguration is thus an opening of the heavens like the baptism, a 'tearing open', as Mark describes it, effected by the Spirit of God: not the dove this time but the presence of Moses and Elijah and the cloud; not the water but the splendour of light on the mountain.[63]

Yet in one sense, the symbolism of the baptism and transfiguration seems to work in opposing ways. The baptism is a *descent* into the waters while the transfiguration involves an *ascent* up the mountain. Mark leaves the enigma of Jesus' baptism until later in the Gospel. After the third passion and resurrection prediction (10:32–4), it becomes clear that Jesus understands baptism as a symbol, along with the cup, of his descent into rejection and death, his identification with sin and suffering.[64] Significantly, it is James and John, two of the three witnesses of the transfiguration, who, perhaps on that basis, request seats of honour in the coming reign of God. To them Jesus throws down the challenge: 'Are you able to drink the cup which I myself drink, or to be baptized with the baptism in which I am baptized?' (10:38). The point is more explicit in Matthew's account of the baptism, but it is also implied in Mark that Jesus descends into sin and suffering as part of his obedience to the Father, submerging himself in the depths of the human condition. The baptism is thus the first indication of the shadow of the cross in Mark's Gospel, part of the 'way of the Lord' (1:3), although the reader does not yet perceive it.[65] Jesus' descent into the water is symbolic of his whole ministry, a ministry that climaxes in his death on the cross – the nadir, the lowest point, of his descent into rejection and death. The divine voice interprets the baptism in two ways: it reveals that Jesus' journey into suffering and sin is the divine will, and it discloses that Jesus will take this path not simply as an ordinary mortal but as the beloved Son of the Father. The descent of the baptism seems a long way from the ascent of the transfiguration.

At the same time, the opposition and parallelism between baptism and transfiguration, between the river and the mountain, coalesce. Jesus descends into the waters and the Spirit descends upon him from heaven. In the transfiguration, Jesus ascends the mountain, the border between heaven and earth, where the cloud overshadows him. Yet Jesus also rises from the water – ascends – and after the transfiguration he descends from the mountain to begin the journey to Jerusalem. In both senses, whether ascending or descending, Jesus takes 'the way of the Lord'. Mark does not explicitly connect the cloud at the transfiguration with the dove at the baptism, although early interpreters believed the connection was close: 'The voice of the Father came from the cloud of the Spirit.'[66] The cloud certainly parallels the dove-like Spirit from heaven at Jesus' baptism, from a narrative perspective, even if Mark does not make explicit the theological association. In any case, the geographical symbols assist to unveil Jesus' identity and mission in relation to God. The one who as Son of Man is 'Lord of the sabbath' (2:28) has traversed the low paths and the high paths, his journey taking him to geographical extremes. By the end of the Gospel, Jesus has plumbed the cosmic heights and depths, revealing his identity as the divine Son and so giving his life as 'a ransom for many' (10:45).

Although the actual location of the transfiguration, as we have seen, is never named in Mark, it is interesting from a symbolic point of view that Mount Hermon has at its foot a chasm with a deep pool of water. According to the Jewish first-century AD historian Josephus, this pool was unable to be plumbed; indeed, it was regarded by pagans in the area as the entrance to the Underworld.[67] Without denying the persistency of the tradition that identifies Mount Tabor as the site of the transfiguration, we can observe how the topography of Hermon accords with Mark's symbolic universe. Jesus ascends the heights and descends into the depths, reaching up to heaven and going down into the horror of hell and darkness:

> My soul is troubled within me; therefore I remember you from the land of Jordan and Hermon, from the small mountain. Deep summons deep at the voice of your cataracts; all your billows and your waves have gone over me. (Ps. 41:7–8, LXX)

This is the mysterious and circuitous path that the Lord's way takes, from height to depth, and only the beloved Son is fit to take it.

After the transfiguration, the third moment of epiphany is the death and resurrection of Jesus.[68] At the beginning of the passion narrative, in the context of the plot to kill Jesus, the unnamed woman who anoints Jesus' head seems to possess an understanding of his death and royal status that his disciples, particularly the twelve, lamentably lack (14:1–11).[69] A little later and on another mountain, the Mount of Olives, Jesus will again take Peter, James and John aside – this time to face in obedience, through the power of prayer, his horrifying death and overcome his revulsion at what awaits him (14:32–42). Once more, Jesus reveals his identity on a mountain, this time paradoxically in intense suffering and anguish,

and once again the inner three disciples fail, for all their efforts, to comprehend. Both mountains – the mount of transfiguration and the Mount of Olives
– are equally revealing of Jesus' identity and the fallibility of his disciples.[70]

In a similar way, the actual manner of Jesus' death has overtones of an
epiphany. Jesus dies not with a sense of confident assurance (as in Luke's
account, Luke 23:46) but with a cry of dereliction on his lips, given both in
Jesus' mother tongue, Aramaic, and in Greek: 'My God, my God, why have
you forsaken me?' (15:34). Some have assumed that, because Jesus is
quoting the opening words of Psalm 22, a psalm of the righteous sufferer,
his final utterance is really evoking the whole psalm, and particularly the
ending with its note of praise and thanksgiving (22:21–31).[71] But such a
supposition misses the point and is in danger of domesticating the stark-
ness of the Markan narrative.[72] The ending of the psalm is not ultimately
irrelevant, given the message of the resurrection in the next chapter, but
it is not immediately relevant to Jesus' death. Mark's story here, as in all
the Gospels, is highly stylized – not written as a journalistic account, but
displaying the inner meaning of the outer event. Difficult as it may be to
grasp, Jesus' cry, for Mark, implies the very real separation of the Son
from the Father. The abandonment is more than a fleeting emotion on
Jesus' part: the divine voice which has spoken out directly at the baptism
and transfiguration now remains terrifyingly silent.[73] Yet Jesus has
already chosen this separation knowingly and willingly, though not without struggle and anguish, as his prayer at Gethsemane indicates
(14:32–42). Just as at the baptism he descends into the waters of the
Jordan and ascends to the opening of the heavens – the dove and the
divine voice – so now he descends symbolically into the waters of sin, suffering, evil, desolation and death. This represents 'the lowest depths of the
hiddenness of the Son of God'.[74] For the sake of the sinful and the suffering, the Son yields up to God more even than his life; he surrenders the
presence of the Father whose will he has obeyed in all things. Here Mark
shows in the starkest of terms 'the oneness of Jesus with humanity ... in
which he shares human despair to the full'.[75] Jesus takes upon himself the
despair, alienation and lostness of humankind.

Yet there is another, paradoxical sense in which the 'voice' of God is not
utterly silent in this narrative, at least to the attentive ear. The two apocalyptic signs may be said to represent that voice, though muted and
ambiguous.[76] The three-hour darkness is often taken as a symbol of divine
judgement and the ending of the old order (see Exod. 10:21–3),[77] but it is
just as likely to be symbolic of absence and mourning: the Father mourn-

ing the death and separation of the Son (see Amos 8:9–10).[78] Indeed, both elements may be present, the divine voice expressing anger as well as grief. Immediately after Jesus' death (15:37), Mark uses the same imagery of tearing open as at the baptism, although this time it is not the heavens but the veil of the temple (15:38, using the same verb, *schizein*, as at 1:10). While this could signify God's judgement on the old order of things, a judgement associated already with Jesus' presence in the temple (11:12–21; 13:2; 14:58), it is better read – at least in its primary meaning – as a radical sign of opening: Jesus' death gives unlimited access to the inner sanctum, the Holy of Holies.[79] The tearing open at the horizontal level may seem opposed to the vertical tearing at the baptism, but both really express the same idea. With Jesus' extraordinary death, open access between heaven and earth is assured; God has indeed torn open the heavens and come down (Isa. 64:1).[80] As a consequence, the death of Jesus 'marks the turning point of the ages'.[81]

That the cross is divinely sanctioned is confirmed in the words of the centurion immediately after Jesus' death: 'Truly this was God's Son' (14:39).[82] This Roman soldier is the last person we would expect to make such a declaration – the only time in Mark's Gospel that a human being recognizes Jesus' sonship. It parallels the divine voice at the baptism and transfiguration, as well as Jesus' own voice at his trial. Admittedly in Mark's story it is often the unexpected people who possess insight, while the insiders remain relatively blind. This is true of the presence of the Galilean women standing at a distance (15:40–1), and Jesus' burial by Joseph of Arimathea, a member of the Jewish council (15:42–6), all of whom contrast markedly with the absent twelve.[83] Even so, it is extraordinary that the one who has crucified Jesus recognizes his identity – and particularly in the context of horror, darkness and death.

But what is it that the Roman soldier sees in Jesus' death to lead him to such a conclusion? At a surface level, the scene reveals nothing but a man dying with a sense of anguish that his God has abandoned him. Of the two apocalyptic signs, only the three-hour period of darkness is accessible to the centurion, the rending of the veil being outside his awareness.[84] It is almost unimaginable that the soldier should recognize not just an innocent victim but the beloved Son in whom the Father takes delight, the one whose coming tears open the heavens, whose glory flashes from the mountain, whose words above all others are to be heeded. In Markan terms, however, what happens is a miracle: only through divine revelation can this Gentile outsider discern in that appalling death, even in its pain and dereliction, God's Son. Jesus' identity is not lost at this point; indeed, for Mark, it is most clearly visible in his act of obedience to the Father and solidarity with a sinful, suffering world. In a situation that bespeaks only the absence of God – violence, suffering, pain, rejection, death – Mark indicates the vibrant presence of God, a presence predicated entirely on Jesus' unique identity. This is the paradox of Mark's understanding of the cross: Jesus' death reveals that God is to be found precisely in those places where, to all intents and purposes, God is absent.

The centre of Mark's Gospel, as we have already seen, consists of a diptych: two portraits of Jesus that depict his identity. At Caesarea Philippi there is a revelation of Jesus as the crucified Son of Man; on the mount of transfiguration there is a revelation of his future glory and true identity. So too the closing scenes of Mark's Gospel present a similar pattern. The death of Jesus, in the first scene, sets forth the suffering and rejection of the Son of Man. This is followed, in the second scene, by the epiphany at the empty tomb (16:1–8). Ironically, this takes place after the burial which should end the whole story of Jesus, and after the heavy stone has been pressed against the mouth of the tomb, emphasizing in human terms the absolute finality of death. At the beginning, middle and end of the Gospel, life and death are thus interwoven, the victory of life emerging only through the paths of the dead.

Perhaps not surprisingly, there are a number of parallels between the transfiguration and the empty tomb story. These similarities do not imply that the two stories are identical or belong to the same genre,[85] but they do indicate that Mark has shaped the moments of epiphany in his Gospel so that they cohere with one another. On the mountain, Jesus is present with his clothing transformed and radiant, in the company of two heavenly figures and with three disciples who respond in fear and incomprehension. At the empty tomb is a young man, a heavenly figure in white clothing – the garb of heaven – in company with the women, three disciples who, like Peter at the transfiguration, are afraid and do not know how to respond. Just as Peter makes an incomprehensible response to the presence of Moses and Elijah, so the women disciples take to their heels and run, too overcome to speak a word (16:8), bringing the Gospel of Mark to its abrupt end.[86] And, just as at the transfiguration three (male) disciples are instructed to listen to the Son – though not to tell until after the resurrection – so now three (female) disciples are enjoined to listen and then to 'go, tell' (16:7). The women do not succeed any better than their male counterparts, though perhaps their fear, like that of Peter, James and John on the mountain, is closer to awe than fright.[87] Yet the reaction of both groups is in one sense perfectly understandable. Not until they see Jesus in Galilee ('there you will see him', 16:7), will the two Marys and Salome finally understand, just as, at the transfiguration, Peter, James and John will not understand until after the resurrection (9:9).

Both on the cross and at the empty tomb – in the last words of Jesus and in the young man's message ('he is not here') – the reader thus confronts a painful absence and learns that it is paradoxically the manifestation of a deeper presence. The theme of presence-in-absence is found in both the crucifixion and resurrection narratives, where Jesus' death and the empty tomb convey a profound and tangible sense of absence. Yet the words of the centurion and the message of the angel manifest the same set of oppositions: life in place of death, beauty in place of ugliness, union instead of separation, joy and hope overriding abandonment and despair. The heavens have been torn open, God's self-revealing has taken place in Jesus' life, death and resurrection. It is the beloved Son who suffers and dies, who experiences the Father's abandonment, whose crucified body is laid in the tomb. Not just an ordinary human being, but the one who is uniquely loved by God, who teaches the words of God, who unveils the revelation of God on the basis of his identity, whose life and death mysteriously manifest the divine splendour, even in the deepest moments of desolation and darkness. Absence and presence work paradoxically to reveal the radical nature of God's reign, the intermingling of suffering and glory. Lying at the heart of Mark's Gospel, the transfiguration encapsulates this paradox: the revealing of the Son in light and glory as he commences his portentous journey to Jerusalem.

The transfiguration in the Gospel of Mark is, in part, an apocalyptic revelation of the future coming of the Son of Man in glory, a 'premonition of the New Creation'.[88] It is equally concerned to display Jesus' identity arching across the earthly and the heavenly. This selfhood, as revealed on the cross, at the empty tomb, in his future appearances in Galilee and at his parousia, is something he possesses from the beginning of the Gospel: in his baptism, his proclaiming of the reign of God, and the words and deeds of his ministry. What is extraordinary is the way Mark links baptism, transfiguration, crucifixion, resurrection and parousia. All these moments of epiphany are connected inextricably to the cross, just as suffering, humiliation, rejection and death are joined to the manifestation of beauty and glory. For Mark, the mount of transfiguration and the Mount of Olives belong together as equally revealing of Jesus' identity and God's self-giving glory. By the end of the Gospel we cannot see Jesus as the beloved Son except in relation to the way of the cross and the transfiguration. Mark's point is not just that Jesus engages radically with human suffering but rather that the beloved Son, revealed in heavenly glory and beauty on the mountain as the harbinger of God's future, and the suffering Son of Man, dying in desolation on the cross, are one and the same person.

Notes

1 For F. J. Moloney (*The Gospel of Mark: A Commentary*, Hendrickson, Peabody, MA, 2002, 178), the transfiguration has a double message: Jesus' relationship with God and the fragility of the disciples.

2 Fletcher-Louis, C. H. T., 'The Revelation of the Sacral Son of Man: The Genre, History of Religions Context and the Meaning of the Transfiguration', in Avemarie, F. and Lichtenberger, H. (eds), *Auferstehung – Resurrection*, J. C. B. Mohr (Paul Siebeck), Tübingen, 2001, 254–6.

3 The saying at 9:1, though difficult, makes sense as a bridge statement; Moses, A. D. A., *Matthew's Transfiguration Story and Jewish–Christian Controversy* (ed. S. E. Porter), Sheffield: Sheffield Academic Press, 1996, 95; and Öhler, M., 'Die Verklärung (Mk 9:1–8): Die Ankunft der Herrschaft Gottes auf der Erde', *Novum Testamentum* 38, 1996, 198.

4 Hooker, M. D., *The Gospel According to St. Mark*, A. & C. Black, London, 1991, pp. 251–3.

5 McCurley, F. R., '"and after Six Days" (Mark 9:2): A Semitic Literary Device', *Journal of Biblical Literature* 93, 1974, 77–8.

6 Ibid., 67–81. Origen, *Commentary on Matthew*, 12.36, in McGuckin, J. A., *The Transfiguration of Christ in Scripture and Tradition*, Edwin Mellen, Lewiston, NY, 1986, 155–6, relates this to the six days of creation.

7 See, e.g., Hooker, M. D., '"What Doest Thou Here, Elijah?": A Look at St. Mark's Account of the Transfiguration', in Hurst, L. D. and Wright, N. T. (eds), *The Glory of Christ in the New Testament*, Clarendon, Oxford, 1987, 59–60.

8 Note Mark's use of the strong verb 'to rebuke' (*epitiman*) at 8:30, 32, 33.

9 On the transfiguration and the secrecy theme in Mark, see Perry, J. M., *Exploring the Transfiguration Story*, Sheed & Ward, Kansas City, MO, 1993, 17–28.

10 For Old Testament associations of the mountain, see Donaldson, T. L., *Jesus on the Mountain: A Study in Matthean Theology*, JSOT Press, Sheffield, 1985, 30–50, 82–3.

11 'Sinai' and 'Horeb' mean the one mount of revelation in the wilderness; Mauser, U., *Christ in the Wilderness: The Wilderness Theme in the Second Gospel and its Basis in the Biblical Tradition*, SCM, London, 1963, 117.

12 Thrall, M. E., 'Elijah and Moses in Mark's Account of the Transfiguration', *NTS* 16, 1969–70, 312.

13 Schmidt, T. E., 'The Penetration of Barriers and the Revelation of Christ in the Gospels', *Novum Testamentum* 34, 1992, 236.

14 Some manuscripts add the words 'as snow' but this is unlikely to be original.

15 Heil, J. P., *The Transfiguration of Jesus: Narrative Meaning and Function of Mark 9:2–8, Matt 17:1–8 and Luke 9:28–36*, Editrice Pontificio Istituto Biblico, Rome, 2000, 156.

16 Juel, D. H., *Mark*, Augsburg, Minneapolis, MN, 1990, 127.

17 'Transfiguration' is from the Latin *transfiguratus est*; the Greek *metamorphosis* means a change in bodily form; Fossum, J. E., 'Ascensio, Metamorphosis: The "Transfiguration" of Jesus in the Synoptic Gospels', in Fossum, J. E., *The Image of the Invisible God: Essays on the Influence of Jewish Mysticism on Early Christology* (N.T.O.A. 30), Vandenhoeck & Ruprecht, Göttingen, 1995, 82, regards the translation 'was transfigured' as unfortunate.

18 Ziesler, J. A., 'The Transfiguration Story and the Markan Soteriology', *Expository Times* 81, 1970, 266. So Boobyer, G. H., *St. Mark and the Transfiguration Story*, T. & T. Clark, Edinburgh, 1942, 65–6.

19 The verb 'transfigured' is a 'divine passive', to avoid the divine name; Heil, *op. cit.*, 77, 155–6.

20 *Shekinah* is used in later Judaism for the visible yet mysterious manifestation of God's glory.

21 McGuckin, *op. cit.*, 18.

22 Boobyer, *op. cit.*, 48–87, argues that all the transfiguration details point to the parousia.

23 Marcus, J., *The Way of the Lord: Christological Exegesis of the Old Testament in the Gospel of Mark*, Westminster/John Knox, Louisville, KY, 1992, 83–4.

24 For the link between 9:1 and Moses and Elijah, see Chilton, B. D., 'The Transfiguration: Dominical Assurance and Apostolic Vision', *New*

Testament Studies 27, 1981, 123, and McGuckin, *op. cit.*, 69–70.

25 Philo, *Questions on Genesis* (trans. R. Marcus) (Loeb Classical Library vol. Supplement I of 12), Harvard University Press, Cambridge, MA, 1979, 1.86. In some Jewish traditions (e.g. the second-century BC Ezekiel the Tragedian), Moses' ascent is his enthronement as king and prophet; Marcus, *op. cit.*, 84–7.

26 Ramsay, M., *The Glory of God and the Transfiguration of Christ*, 2nd edn, Darton, Longman & Todd, London, 1967, 114–15.

27 Fossum, *op. cit.*, 88–9.

28 Hooker, 'Transfiguration', 68.

29 John Chrysostom, *Homily 56 on Matthew 17*, 1, in McGuckin, op. cit., 174.

30 See Caird, G. B., 'The Transfiguration', *Expository Times* 67, 1955–6, 292: Peter 'simply blurted out the first thing that came into his head'.

31 For a summary of the various suggestions, see Heil, *op. cit.*, 116–18.

32 For this view, see Boobyer, op. cit., 76–9, and Riesenfeld, H., *Jésus Transfiguré: L'arrière-plan du récit Évangélique de la Transfiguration de Notre-Seigneur*, Munksgaard, Copenhagen, 1947, 265–80.

33 See, e.g., Thrall, *op. cit.*, 308–9 and Öhler, *op. cit.*, 208–9.

34 So Heil, *op. cit.*, 118–27, who thinks the audience finds resonances in all three views.

35 McGuckin, *op. cit.*, 72, speaks of a 'somewhat foolish and misplaced' offer.

36 Taylor, V., *The Gospel According to St. Mark*, Macmillan, London, 1952, 391.

37 Note the echo of the word 'here' (*hôde*) from 9:1.

38 The adjective *kalos* originally meant beautiful rather than good; both aspects are present here.

39 Tertullian, *Against Marcion*, 4.22, in McGuckin, *op. cit.*, 252.

40 van Iersel, B. M. F., *Mark: A Reader-Response Commentary*, Sheffield Academic Press, Sheffield, 1998, 128, exaggerates when he compares this to the worship of the golden calf.

41 Augustine, *Homily 28*, in McGuckin, *op. cit.*, 276.

42 On Jesus' bodily transpositions in the Gospels, see Ward, G., 'Bodies: The Displaced Body of Jesus Christ', in Millbank, J., Pickstock, C. and Ward, G. (eds), *Radical Orthodoxy*, Routledge, London, 1999.

43 It is unlikely that the disciples are included in the cloud; see Öhler, *op. cit.*, 210–11.

44 At one point Moses cannot enter the tent of meeting because the cloud

'overshadowed' it (Exod. 40:34–5); see Schulz, S., *'Episkiaziô'*, in Kittel, G. and Friedrich, G. (eds), *Theological Dictionary of the New Testament*, vol. 7, Eerdmans, Grand Rapids, MI, 1971, 399–400. The verb *episkiazein* sounds similar to *skênê*, 'tent'.

45 Oepke, A., *'Nephelê'*, in Kittel, G. (ed.), *Theological Dictionary of the New Testament*, vol. 4, Eerdmans, Grand Rapids, MI, 1967, 908; Cranfield, C. E. B., *The Gospel According to Saint Mark: An Introduction and Commentary*, Cambridge University Press, Cambridge, 1959, 292. For Heil, *op. cit.*, 129–49, the cloud is a vehicle but this is unlikely given that they do not arrive in it.

46 Origen, *Commentary on Matthew*, 12:42, and Proclus of Constantinople, *Oration* 8, both in McGuckin, *op. cit.*, 162, 185.

47 The verb, to reveal, (*apokalyptein*) means literally 'to uncover'.

48 Mauser, *op. cit.*, 114.

49 Kee, H. C., 'The Transfiguration in Mark: Epiphany or Apocalyptic Vision', in Reumann, J. (ed.), *Understanding the Sacred Text: Essays in Honor of Morton S. Enslin on the Hebrew Bible and Christian Beginnings*, Judson Press, Valley Forge, PA, 1972, 139, 144, 148; Stegner, W. R., 'The Use of Scripture in Two Narratives of Early Jewish Christianity (Matth 4.1–11; Mark 9.2–8)', in Evans, C. A. and Sanders, J. A. (eds), *Early Christian Interpretation of the Scriptures of Israel: Investigations and Proposals*, Sheffield Academic Press, Sheffield, 1997, 111; and Öhler, *op. cit.*, 200–1, 209, 213; on Mark's editing of the original story, along these lines, see Best, E., 'The Markan Redaction of the Transfiguration', in Livingstone, E. A. (ed.), *International Congress on Biblical Studies*, Akademie, Berlin, 1982.

50 Ziesler, *op. cit.*, describes the transfiguration as 'a piece of Markan soteriology'.

51 It is possible that there is an allusion to Isaac here (Gen. 22); see McCurley, *op. cit.*, 78–80.

52 Kee, *op. cit.*, 144, 148–9, argues that Jesus' glory is not divine but, like Moses, borrowed.

53 Assuming 'Son of God' is part of the original Markan text.

54 Thompson, M. M., *The Promise of the Father: Jesus and God in the New Testament*, Westminster/John Knox, Louisville, KY, 2000, 91.

55 *Ibid.*, 92.

56 The overtones of intimacy should not be pressed; see Barr, J., *'Abba* Isn't Daddy', *Journal of Theological Studies* 39, 1988, and Thompson, *op. cit.*, 90.

57 See Schweizer, E., *Jesus*, SCM, London, 1971, 13–51.

58 Fletcher-Louis, *op. cit.*, 248.

59 Barton, S. C., 'The Transfiguration of Christ According to Mark and Matthew: Christology and Anthropology', in Avemarie, F. and Lichtenberger, H. (eds), *Auferstehung – Resurrection*, J.C.B. Mohr (Paul Siebeck), Tübingen, 2001, 241–2.

60 Marcus, *op. cit.*, 72.

61 Hooker, *St. Mark*, 218.

62 McGuckin, *op. cit.*, 26.

63 Myers, C., *Binding the Strong Man: A Political Reading of Mark's Story of Jesus*, Orbis, Maryknoll, NY, 1990, 251.

64 McGuckin, *op. cit.* and Caird, *op. cit.*, 292.

65 The background to this Markan motif is probably Second-Isaiah; so Marcus, *op. cit.*, 48.

66 See, e.g., Hilary of Poitiers, *Commentary on Matthew* 17:3, and John of Damascus, *Akrostich*, 18, both in McGuckin, *op. cit.*, 258, 222.

67 Josephus, *Jewish War*, I.404; see Fletcher-Louis, *op. cit.*, 267–74.

68 Myers, *op. cit.*, 390–2.

69 Heil, *op. cit.*, 188.

70 McGuckin, *op. cit.*, 65, speaks of the parallel 'between the glorious epiphany of the Metamorphosis and the sorrowful epiphany of the Agony in Gethsemane'; see also Kenny, A., 'The Transfiguration and the Agony in the Garden', *Catholic Biblical Quarterly* 19, 1957, 444–5.

71 See Nineham, D. E., *Saint Mark*, Penguin Books, Harmondsworth, 1963, 428–9, and Senior, D., *The Passion of Jesus in the Gospel of Mark*, Michael Glazier, Wilmington, DE, 1984, 123–4.

72 Brown, R. E., *The Death of the Messiah – From Gethsemane to the Grave: A Commentary on the Passion Narratives in the Four Gospels*, 2 vols, Doubleday, New York, 1994, 1049–51, argues that the cry expresses anguish from 'an utterly forlorn Jesus' who is 'isolated and estranged' (1050).

73 Van Iersel, *op. cit.*, 189, and Myers, *op. cit.*, 389.

74 Cranfield, *op. cit.*, 458.

75 Hooker, *St. Mark*, 375.

76 For Brown, *op. cit.*, 1044, the cry – which, he argues, is uttered once – is an apocalyptic sign.

77 *Ibid.*, vol. 2, 1035–6.

78 Schweizer, E., *The Good News According to Mark: A Commentary on the Gospel* (trans. D. H. Madvig), SPCK, London, 1970, 352.

79 This could be the inner curtain to the Holy of Holies or the outer veil between the porch and the sanctuary. Josephus, *Jewish War*, V.212–14, says that the veil of the sanctuary was decorated in bright colours with a picture of the vault of heaven; see Schmidt, *op. cit.*, 229.

80 Evans, C. A., *Mark* 8:27–16:20 vol. 34B, (ed. R. P. Martin), Thomas Nelson, Nashville, TN, 2001, 508–9, sees the torn veil as the result of Jesus' death shout at 15:37.

81 Moloney, *op. cit.*, 328.

82 The Greek could mean 'a son of God', but this does not fit Mark's evangelical purpose at this point.

83 The woman who anoints Jesus' head at the beginning of the passion recognizes a kingship that will be manifest ironically in his crucifixion (14:3–9); this incident parallels the holy women at the cross.

84 Against this, see Jackson, H. M., 'The Death of Jesus in Mark and the Miracle from the Cross', *New Testament Studies* 33, 1987, 22–32, who argues that the centurion does see the rending of the veil, which is caused by Jesus' last cry.

85 So Dodd, C. H., 'The Appearances of the Risen Christ: An Essay in Form-Criticism of the Gospels', in Nineham, D. E. (ed.), *Studies in the Gospels: Essays in Memory of R. H. Lightfoot*, Blackwell, Oxford, 1957.

86 Assuming, with the majority, that the Gospel ends at 16:8. Against this, see Schweizer, *Mark*, 365–7, and Evans, *op. cit.*, 550–1.

87 So Lightfoot, R. H., *The Gospel Message of St. Mark*, Clarendon, Oxford, 87–9; see also Magness, J. L., *Sense and Absence: Structure and Suspension in the Ending of Mark's Gospel*, Scholars Press, Atlanta, GA, 1986, 87–105.

88 Wink, W., 'Mark 9:2–8', *Interpretation* 36, 1982, 65.

2
The Transfiguration in Matthew

17:1 And after six days, Jesus took Peter, James, and John his brother, and bore them up to a high mountain in private. 2 And he was transfigured before them, and his face shone like the sun and his clothes became white like the light. 3 And behold there appeared to them Moses and Elijah talking together with him. 4 Peter said to Jesus in response, 'Lord, it is good for us to be here; if you wish, I will make here three tents, one for you, one for Moses and one for Elijah.' 5 While he was still speaking behold a bright cloud overshadowed them, and behold a voice out of the cloud said: 'This is my beloved Son, in whom I am well pleased; listen to him.' 6 And the disciples when they heard fell on their faces and were very afraid. 7 Then Jesus approached and touching them said, 'Rise up and do not fear.' 8 Having raised their eyes they saw no-one except Jesus alone. 9 And as they were descending the mountain, Jesus instructed them, 'Tell no-one of the vision until the Son of Man has been raised from the dead.'

(Matt. 17:1–9)

Matthew's story of the transfiguration tells of Jesus' metamorphosis in language that is redolent with symbols of light. Jesus' face shines like the sun and the overshadowing cloud is bright, blazing with light. This splendour betokens Jesus' identity as the divine Son, a splendour that stands in the tradition of, yet far exceeds, the greatness of Moses on Mount Sinai. At the same time, Matthew is concerned with the vocation of the Church, symbolized particularly in Peter. Jesus, who is Lord of the Church, approaches the overawed disciples with tenderness and understanding, and raises them up with reassuring words. After the disappearance of the heavenly signs – Moses and Elijah, the light, the cloud and the voice – and during the descent down the mountain, Jesus reveals to the disciples that what they have witnessed is no less than a vision of God's future. This future is transmitted from the past by the symbolic importance of Moses and anticipated in the present by the majestic yet compassionate figure of Jesus, the beloved Son.

For the most part, Matthew follows the wider Markan structure of the journey to Jerusalem (16:13–20:34), with its distinctive architecture of three passion and resurrection predictions (16:21; 17:22–3; 20:17–19; cf. 17:12). Here too, Matthew makes the material his own, expanding the journey to Jerusalem (e.g. 18:12–35; 19:1–16) and bringing his own distinctive emphases to bear on the Markan narrative. In line with his theological emphasis on the Church, for example, Matthew is less critical of the disciples than Mark. As a result, he omits the healing of the blind man at the beginning of the journey, with its suggestion of the blindness of the disciples, and modifies the story of the disciples quarrelling over greatness in the community (18:1–5). Moreover, Matthew's depiction of the way of the cross places the emphasis on Jesus' obedience to the Father rather than his embrace of powerlessness, as in Mark. These differences affect considerably our reading of Matthew's transfiguration.

The Matthæan transfiguration is closely connected to the story at Caesarea Philippi, both episodes concerned with the revealing of Jesus' identity. As with Mark, these scenes represent for Matthew the evangelical and literary heart of the Gospel. A closer inspection shows important differences in the way Mark and Matthew present the material. Matthew 16:13–17:13 is a unit but, rather than comprising two panels that depict Jesus' identity, it has four scenes, each of which deals with the twin themes of Christology and Church. The new community is built on the figure of Peter, whose declaration of faith at Caesarea Philippi is the result of divine revelation, thus making him the 'rock' of the Church (16:16–18).[1] Just as Peter makes a 'you are' statement of Jesus, so too does Jesus of Peter, each naming the other and creating the basis for the building of the Church; a Markan story about Christology thus becomes in Matthew's hands a story about the Church. The result is that, in the transfiguration, Matthew is as much concerned with the conversion of the disciples as with the revelation of Jesus.[2]

The four episodes in this mid-section of Matthew's Gospel have a more or less similar structure. Each deals with Jesus' identity, the consequent identity of the Church, and reassurance for the future destiny of the community. Each episode, in other words, concerns Christology, Church and eschatology, the three being inextricably linked. The promise about 'some standing here', who will not taste death until the coming of the Son of Man (16:28), is more integrally related to the previous episode than in Mark, becoming the climax of Jesus' invitation to discipleship and leading directly into the transfiguration. This is the same Son of Man who will rise from

Table 2.1

Episode 1: Revelation of Church at Caesarea Philippi (16:13–20)	• *Jesus' Identity:* Jesus as Son of Man, Messiah, Son of living God, excelling all prophets, including Elijah and John the Baptist • *Discipleship:* Founding of Church on Peter and his faith confession • *Reassurance:* Final triumph of Church over powers of Underworld
Episode 2: Revelation of Way of Cross (16:21–8)	• *Jesus' Identity:* Jesus as suffering, dying and risen one • *Discipleship:* Disciples called to follow way of cross • *Reassurance:* Path through death leads to life, glory and Son of Man's reign
Episode 3: Revelation of Transfiguration on Mountain (17:1–8)	• *Jesus' Identity:* Jesus as radiant, transfigured Son • *Discipleship:* Fearful disciples fall on their faces • *Reassurance:* Disciples reassured by approach of Christ and promise of resurrection
Episode 4: Revelation of Jesus' Suffering as Part of Restoration (17:10–13)	• *Jesus' Identity:* Necessity of suffering of Son of Man, prefigured in Elijah and John the Baptist • *Discipleship:* Disciples question Jesus about the end time and role of Elijah • *Reassurance:* Restoration of all things already begun

the dead (17:9), the title forming a circle around the transfiguration.[3] The command to secrecy at 17:9 is transitional, leading into Jesus' conversation with the disciples as they descend the mountain (see Table 2.1).

In telling the tale of the transfiguration, Matthew is content to follow the broad contours of Mark's account. Its position in the plan of the Gospel, the overall plot, the response of the main characters, and the theological meaning are similar. Yet it would be a mistake to confuse Mark's and Matthew's versions or to assume that the variations are insignificant. There are important differences between the two accounts, both in detail and theological emphasis. Indeed, in some ways, Matthew's story is smoother and more complete than Mark's – less abrupt and stark.[4] The Old Testament background is even more prominent in Matthew's version, presenting a number of overlapping themes.[5] Apart from minor alterations, Matthew has changed the Markan outline of the transfiguration narrative in one particular way: he locates the disciples' fear *after* the divine voice rather than before it. As in Mark's account, the first two heavenly signs – transfiguration, appearance of Moses and Elijah – are interpreted by the second two, the bright cloud and the heavenly voice. The disciples' reaction thus surrounds the revelation of the cloud and the voice. In line with the focus on the Church, Matthew re-locates the disciples' fear in order to strengthen the symbolic role of the disciples in this scene.[6] The story can be structured as shown in Table 2.2.

Matthew is the only evangelist to categorize the literary form of the transfiguration story. In the descent from the mountain, Jesus calls it a 'vision' – literally, something that is seen (*horama*, 17:9). This description can be misleading and is not as elucidating as it appears. To the modern mind, a vision is a subjective, internal experience unavailable to others and perhaps the product of the imagination. But in Matthew, the transfiguration is an objective event, available to the eyes – and ears – of the three disciples.[7] The word 'vision' in the biblical world means something that can be tangibly seen, an appearance or spectacle, implying something of a heightened or even heavenly nature.[8] Most likely, what we have here in Matthew is in part an apocalyptic vision and in part an epiphany whose symbolic background lies in Moses' ascent of Mount Sinai.[9]

Matthew begins his story with a time reference, identical to Mark's Gospel, indicting that the transfiguration occurs six days after the conversation at Caesarea Philippi (17:1). The emphasis on Moses throughout Matthew's Gospel, as apparent in the five discourses (which parallel the five books of Moses in the Old Testament),[10] is enough to make the link with Moses and Sinai. The first time Moses ascends the mountain, the cloud covers it for six days and only on the seventh does the Lord speak from the cloud. Moses then enters the cloud, climbing higher up the mountain and remaining on the mountain peak for forty days and nights (Exod. 24:15–17). Although the parallelism is not exact in Matthew, the allusions are strong.[11] On the seventh day Jesus, like Moses, ascends the mountain and enters the awesome presence of God. Thus, the revelation on the

Table 2.2

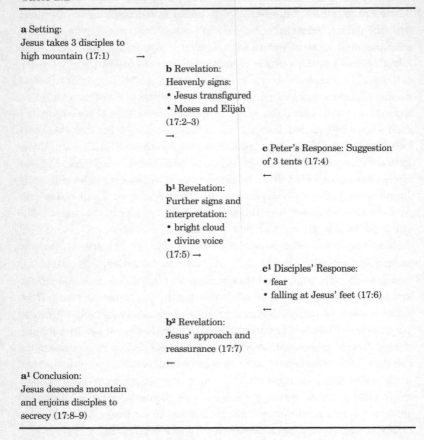

a Setting:
Jesus takes 3 disciples to
high mountain (17:1) →

      b Revelation:
      Heavenly signs:
      • Jesus transfigured
      • Moses and Elijah
      (17:2–3)
      →

            c Peter's Response: Suggestion
            of 3 tents (17:4)
            ←

      b¹ Revelation:
      Further signs and
      interpretation:
      • bright cloud
      • divine voice
      (17:5) →

            c¹ Disciples' Response:
            • fear
            • falling at Jesus' feet (17:6)
            ←

      b² Revelation:
      Jesus' approach and
      reassurance (17:7)
      ←

a¹ Conclusion:
Jesus descends mountain
and enjoins disciples to
secrecy (17:8–9)

mount of transfiguration parallels that of Sinai and the giving of the law. Furthermore, the reference to six days strengthens the link between Matthew's story of the transfiguration and the two preceding episodes, where Jesus' self-revelation leads to the constitution of the Church as the people of God.

The Sinai parallels extend to the three disciples. On his first ascent up the mountain, Moses is accompanied by three men, Aaron, Nadab and Abihu (as well as seventy elders); later Moses makes the last part of the journey with only Joshua for company. So in Matthew, the three disciples – Peter, James and John – accompany Jesus up the mountain as he enters the presence of God. These same three disciples have already played an important part in Matthew's Gospel. Jesus has called them, along with

Andrew, from their occupation as fishermen (4:18–22). In company with
the twelve, they have listened to Jesus' teaching and witnessed his healing
ministry. Appointed as apostles, they have been sent out with Jesus' own
authority to heal and exorcize (10:1–4).[12] As disciples, they represent
Jesus' true family who share the same desire to 'do the will of my Father
in heaven' (12:50; see Mark 3:35).[13] Yet for all the similarities, Matthew's
characterization of the disciples is different from Mark's. The twelve are
more prominent and portrayed more sympathetically, their efforts to
understand attended by some success. Matthew omits Mark's reference to
their hardness of heart after the first feeding story and Jesus' walking on
the water (see Mark 6:52; Matt. 14:22–32); instead the disciples worship
him and recognize his identity (Matt. 14:33). Matthew prefers to speak of
them having 'little faith' rather than none (6:30; 8:26; 14:31; 16:8). He also
gives more emphasis to the character of Peter, as in his walking on the
water (14:28–31), his faith confession at Caesarea Philippi and the role he
plays in the Church (16:16–18). As a result, the inner group of three is
somewhat less prominent than in Mark; they are not singled out at the
raising of the synagogue leader's daughter (9:18–26), nor in Jesus' apocalyptic discourse (Matthew 24).[14] Although the three are mentioned at
Gethsemane and witness Jesus' struggle, the accent is more on Peter than
the other two (26:40). The same is true of the transfiguration. In the light
of what has gone before, the emphasis is on the disciples' role – especially
Peter's – as representative of the new Israel, the Church.

The other symbols of the transfiguration are equally imposing. As elsewhere in the Bible, the mountain is a sacred place associated with revelation, perched on the boundary between heaven and earth. Matthew presupposes Old Testament associations of the mountain with salvation, the
banquet of the end time, where peace, prosperity and joy will reign and
suffuse the earth (Isa. 11:6–9; 25:6–10a; Ezek. 47:1–12). The mountain is
the place of God's dwelling on Sion (Ps. 25:8; 87:1–2; Wis. 9:8), the
revelation of God's righteousness and love. It is also, as we have seen, pre-
eminently associated with the gift of the law. In Matthew's Gospel, however,
mountains have particular significance. The Matthæan Jesus ascends six
mountains throughout the Gospel (including the transfiguration), each
occasion numinous and cosmic, associated with revelation.[15]

The first is the 'mount of temptation', where the devil takes Jesus up a
high mountain (*paralambanei … eis horos hypsêlon*, 4:8). There he shows
Jesus 'all the kingdoms of the world and their glory (*doxa*)', offering him
sovereignty, providing that Jesus will 'fall down and worship' him (4:9).

The wording is strikingly similar to the transfiguration, where Jesus takes the three disciples up the mountain (17:1) and later they 'fall down' on their faces before him (17:9). Only in these two contexts in Matthew is the mountain referred to as 'high'. The devil attempts to appropriate divine sovereignty, demanding the worship that belongs to God alone; later in the Gospel the same worship will be given to Jesus by his disciples. Thus, the transfiguration serves as a 'positive counterimage' to the temptation story.[16]

The second is the 'mount of teaching', where Jesus delivers the Sermon on the Mount (5:1; 8:1). Here the associations with Moses are prominent, both in the setting and content of Jesus' teaching, which is concerned with the interpretation of the law in everyday life. Jesus is the definitive interpreter of Torah, setting his own teaching authority above even the ancients. These aspects makes their way, by association, into the transfiguration story. Just as Moses ascended Mount Sinai to see the divine glory and receive the law – revelation and teaching – so too Jesus ascends the mount of transfiguration, is revealed in glory, and his disciples are instructed to pay heed to his teaching.

The third is the 'mount of feeding', where on two occasions Jesus ascends the mountain in the context of the feeding saga (14:13–16:12). After the first feeding incident, where Jesus has healed and fed the crowd, he departs to a mountain privately in order to pray (*kat' idian*, 14:23; see 17:1). Immediately afterwards, he appears to the frightened disciples on the water who are struggling with a contrary wind, and encourages Peter to walk towards him on the waves (14:25–33). Matthew has already indicated that the boat is a symbol of the Church, the community of disciples, living in an apocalyptic context of trouble and persecution (8:23–7).[17] By the end of this episode, the Lord's calming, reassuring presence leads the disciples to 'worship him', acclaiming him 'truly the Son of God' (14:33). Here admittedly, unlike the transfiguration, the mountain scene precedes Jesus' self-disclosure on the waters, but the two scenes are intimately linked. Jesus' experience of prayer on the mountain emphasizes his communion with the Father which is the source of his identity (11:27). Not long after, we find Jesus again beside the Sea of Galilee; this time he ascends the mountain (15:29), where he heals and feeds the crowds (15:29–39). The mount of feeding (though it is also the mount of healing) illustrates that Jesus' ministry of compassion is as significant as his teaching ministry – equally revealing of his divinely authority. Once more in Matthew, the one who is the Messiah in word is also the Messiah in deed, thus demonstrating his authenticity.[18]

After the mount of transfiguration is the Mount of Olives, following the Last Supper (26:30). Here Jesus predicts the disciples' desertion and denial, and goes to Gethsemane in company with Peter, James and John, where he submits to the divine will and is then arrested (26:31–56). The Mount of Olives is the mirror-opposite to the mount of transfiguration.[19] In both Jesus is surrounded by his three closest disciples and in both he reveals his utter dependence on God as Father. Yet one is a place of suffering and struggle, and the other of glory and light. One is characterized by darkness and violence, moving between the private and the public arena, the other is full of radiance and calm, entirely private. One occurs at the lowest point of the Matthæan narrative,[20] the other is both literally and symbolically one of its highest points. In Matthew, both mountains encapsulate Jesus' identity as the Son of God, in his radiance and obedience, his exaltation and humiliation, his glory and suffering. Neither location is possible theologically without the other.

Finally, as the climax to the Gospel, the sixth mountain is the 'mount of commissioning', where the risen Christ appears to the eleven disciples in Galilee. There, on the mountain, he reveals his full identity, no longer hidden, as the one to whom all dominion 'in heaven and on earth' belongs (28:18). This is the same dominion the devil has offered him at the temptation, which he now receives on account of his obedience and suffering. He commissions the Church with its mission to the Gentiles – making disciples and teaching – and promises his abiding presence with his disciples, the Church, for ever (28:19–20). Thus is fulfilled the promise of Emmanuel, 'God with us', at the beginning of the Gospel (1:23; cf. 18:20), recognized ironically not by the leaders of Israel, but by the Gentile Magi (2:1–18).

Looking back from the mountain peak across the panorama of the Gospel, we note three things about Matthew's mountain symbolism. First, the mountain is usually not identified in this Gospel (apart from the Mount of Olives), although it seems to be in the region of Galilee, giving the impression that in most cases it is symbolically the same mountain – the mountain of God. The effect is to link the mountain scenarios throughout the narrative, from the third temptation at the beginning of Jesus' ministry to the transfiguration in the middle and the glorious revelation of the sovereign Christ at the end. Second, each scenario reveals Jesus' identity, the mountain being close to heaven and thus revelatory. Even the mount of temptation reveals Jesus' identity as the divine Son who offers a life of integrity and goodness to the Father. Whether explicitly or not,

Jesus on the mountain speaks and acts as the beloved, well-pleasing Son, the embodiment of divine presence and revelation. This revelation parallels, yet also radically exceeds, that given to Moses on Sinai. Third, the mountain is associated with faith and worship, as exemplified by the disciples. This worship is offered in the first place to God – and initially by Jesus himself on the mount of temptation – but it is later accorded to the risen Christ, the one in whom all sovereignty resides. These three aspects of Matthew's mountain theology colour the way we read the transfiguration.

The powerful use of mountain symbolism gives particular force to the actual metamorphosis of Jesus on the mount of transfiguration (17:2). The language is that of divine action; it is God who transfigures Jesus, unveiling his true identity. Matthew makes three statements at this point (rather than Mark's two): Jesus is metamorphosed, his face shines and his clothes are dazzling white (17:2). Once more, we are speaking of a radical change in Jesus' whole person, not just his face and clothing. The point is accentuated more in Matthew than in Mark with the description of Jesus' face shining 'like the sun' (*hôs hêlios*, 17:2), a description that replaces (and improves) Mark's rather awkward description of bleach. The explicit reference to Jesus' face is absent from Mark's telling but present also in Luke, although Luke's wording is different (Luke 9:29).[21] Once more we can detect the influence of the story of Moses' descent from Mount Sinai, when his face shone so brightly that he had to cover it against the people's dismay (Exod. 34:29–35; see 2 Cor. 3:7–18).[22] The radiance of Jesus' face parallels the radiance of Moses at the giving of the law.[23] More than the depiction of Moses, Matthew 'pictures the transfigured Jesus in the full radiance of heavenly splendor'.[24]

The symbol of light (*phôs*) is an important one in the opening chapters of Matthew's Gospel. It begins with the star that rises in the east to proclaim the birth of a king and to light the way of the wise men to the Christ child (2:1–2, 7–10). Matthew develops the light motif in Jesus' first proclamation of his ministry and the coming reign of God, quoting from Isaiah: 'the people sitting in darkness have seen a great light, and on those seated in the place and shadow of death light has dawned' (Matt. 4:16; Isa. 9:2). Matthew understands this light as the light of God's presence, manifest in Jesus-Emmanuel (Matt. 1:23; cf. Isa. 9:6). Later Matthew will make plain that the same light is to be displayed in the life of disciples (5:14–16; 6:22–3; 10:27). The light shines out of surrounding darkness, illuminating the inner being as well as the outer world.

Matthew, like Mark, makes no explicit mention of glory (*doxa*) in the transfiguration account. But the added emphasis given to the motif of light, along with the reference to glory in the preceding scene (16:27), shows that Matthew presupposes it. In the previous case, glory is found with explicitly apocalyptic overtones: the Son of Man is to return 'in the glory of his Father' as the Judge of the end time. In general, the symbolism of light and luminous faces displays apocalyptic influence. In addition to God, the faces of the righteous in heaven shine with light at the end time, displaying the radiance of union with God and their glorification above earthly trials.[25] In Matthew's Gospel, the righteous too will shine like the sun after the final judgement (13:43). Both glory and light thus belong to God and point to God's eschatological salvation dawning already in the darkness of the world, through the splendour of Christ.

It would be a mistake, however, to read the transfiguration only as an anticipation of Christ's future glory in the resurrection and parousia. The apocalyptic dimension is vital to Matthew's theology but does not exhaust it. The Moses and Mount Sinai symbolism, as we have seen, gives another dimension to the transfiguration, light being associated with epiphanies as well as apocalyptic visions. The God-given light of the old covenant is not just repeated in Jesus' experience but surpassed on the mount of transfiguration, with the advent of the new. God displays Jesus, in his physical presence, as the beloved Son, clothed in divine light, a light that excels the greatest of Old Testament revelation. Yet the light displayed in Jesus' metamorphosis on the mountain is not simply an external clothing, nor even a reflected glory. Rather, it is the outward manifestation of the inner person, as revealed by God. Jesus is shown as he is in his true self, hidden from the eyes of the world, which is also the guise in which he will be more completely revealed in the coming reign (or kingdom) of heaven:

> Christ was transfigured not by receiving something he did not have before, nor by being changed into something he previously was not, but as manifesting to his disciples what he really was, opening their eyes and from blind men making them see again.[26]

Matthew's simile of the sun presents Jesus as the divine dawn, the radiant presence which illuminates the darkness of sin and suffering. In this epiphany, Jesus' true nature is unveiled, becoming 'luminous, transparent to the disciples' gaze'.[27]

Matthew introduces the appearance of Moses and Elijah with the dramatic word 'behold' (17:3) – usually omitted in English translations –

indicating that something of a heightened nature is about to take place. Here Matthew follows the traditional, chronological order of the two names, making their presence less future oriented than in Mark. Nonetheless, many of the same elements are present. Although it is awkward to have Moses and Elijah standing, respectively, for the law and the prophets – given that Moses represents both dimensions – their symbolic significance need not be narrowly interpreted. As major prophets of the Old Testament and champions of the law, Moses and Elijah signify Israel's past, a past that is embedded in Jesus' own spirituality. Both figures are associated (in some sense) with bypassing death, Elijah explicitly so in the biblical account (2 Kgs 2:1–12) and Moses in later Jewish traditions, on account of the strange circumstances of his death and burial (Deut. 34:1–8).[28] Both have direct and startling experiences of God on Mount Sinai/Horeb, particularly Moses at the burning bush (Exod. 3; 24; 34; cf. 1 Kgs 19:1–11).[29]

Elijah is not as consequential a figure for Matthew as he is for Mark. Matthew retains something of Mark's perspective on him as acting as the type of both John the Baptist and Jesus himself, particularly in relation to suffering (17:10–13). Elijah's bypassing of death, moreover, provides a loose type of Jesus' own resurrection. But Moses is of greater import for Matthew. The birth narrative with its massacre of the innocents and the flight into Egypt (2:1–18), the mountain symbolism, the emphasis on the abiding significance of the law (5:17–20), and the five discourses around which the Matthæan narrative turns, all parallel events and themes within the life of Moses. The common material between the stories of Moses and Jesus suggests that Matthew's Jesus acts, in some sense, as the new Moses. Yet Jesus does not give a new law but unveils the true meaning of the law of Moses; indeed, he is the definitive interpreter of Moses, in act as well as word, especially in his life of humility where he 'fulfils all righteousness' (3:15). Even while interpreting him, Jesus speaks with an authority that surpasses Moses (Matt. 5:21–48). Thus the Jesus of Matthew's Gospel is 'at the same time like Moses and greater than Moses',[30] a portrait that, as the transfiguration makes plain, contains no anti-Mosaic polemic. Jesus is more exalted than Moses but stands firmly in the same tradition.[31]

At the transfiguration, Moses and Elijah appear in a subservient role to Jesus, acting as his heavenly attendants. They are not explicitly associated with light as he is, nor are they depicted as his equals. Nothing is said in Matthew's narrative of their appearance that is comparable with Jesus. On the contrary, their presence – with all that their life and witness signify of Israel's election by God – points symbolically to Jesus as the definitive revelation of God. In company with these two great servants of God, therefore, whose life and death point forward to 'the one who is to come' (11:3), Jesus stands as the true Servant of God, chosen beyond all others. The significance of Moses and Elijah, like every other detail of the transfiguration, is fundamentally related to Matthew's Christology. In the end, the figure of Moses, like that of Elijah, is 'absorbed into and transcended by the larger pattern of Son-christology'.[32]

The disciples' response to the transfiguration demonstrates Matthew's understanding of the role of the Church. The first is Peter's suggestion that occurs immediately following the metamorphosis of Jesus' face and clothing (17:4). His request to be permitted to construct three tents (leafy shelters made of branches) is a misunderstanding but not, in Matthew's eyes, a serious one. We have already observed that Matthew's portrait of the twelve is considerably more sympathetic than that of Mark. Peter addresses Jesus as *Kyrie*, meaning 'sir' or 'Lord', a common title for Jesus in Matthew, most often used with heightened meaning ('Lord') in the context of faith,[33] and certainly more appropriate to this sublime context than the Markan 'Rabbi' (Mark 9:5). Matthew's Peter also makes his suggestion in words that are both humble and personal: 'if you wish, I will make ...'. The wording expresses his uncertainty but also his readiness to submit to Jesus' will if his suggestion should prove misguided, just as Jesus will later submit to the Father's will at Gethsemane (26:39, 42). Peter's indecision and humility, coupled with his awareness of how 'good' it is for him and his companions to witness the beauty and splendour of this event, make his proposal seem ambiguous. The fact that Jesus makes no response – and the storyteller no editorial comment (unlike Mark) – but the intervening cloud cuts off Peter's suggestion, indicates to the reader that Peter's notion is well-intentioned but inadequate.

The range of possibilities for Peter's meaning is similar to Mark and similarly difficult to pin down.[34] At least three Old Testament possibilities exist. First, Peter may have in mind the feast of Tabernacles with its custom of dwelling in tents, commemorating the journey through the wilderness in Israel's past (Lev. 23:33–6; Deut. 16:13–15) and pointing to the joy of the last days in the future.[35] Second, Peter may be thinking of the tent of meeting in the wilderness where God spoke to Moses and where the cloud of the divine presence hovered (Exod. 33:7–11; Deut. 31:14–15).[36] Or, third, on the basis of Jesus' clothing, Peter may want to construct the eschatological dwellings of the righteous on the assumption that the end time has arrived,[37] even though Matthew (like Mark) makes no reference to Moses and Elijah's apparel. Given Matthew's strong interest in Moses, we might be inclined to adopt the second of these, although the third is also possible given Matthew's apocalyptic interests. Yet, as we saw with Mark, though these suggestions have a certain plausibility, none entirely works. The feast of Tabernacles would require six tents rather than three (for the three disciples as well), and is the least likely explanation, while for the tent of meeting Peter should propose only one. As for the righteous, it is hard to see why he would imagine that huts made of leafy branches could compare with heavenly lodgings. Most likely Peter wishes to respond in a positive way and is not clear in his own mind – as his hesitation suggests – what the appropriate response should be. His tradition knows of tents, in a number of different contexts, and he grasps at the idea without being clear what he really means, except perhaps to retain the goodness and beauty before it evaporates before his eyes,[38] as well as to commemorate, however feebly, so distinguished a gathering.[39]

There is another dimension to Peter's misunderstanding that makes sense in this context, and illustrates Matthew's divergence from Mark. In the first episode at Caesarea Philippi, following Peter's inspired recognition of Jesus' identity as the divine Son (16:16), Jesus announces that he will build his Church on Peter (16:18) and presents him with the keys (16:19). It is surely significant that Peter in the transfiguration speaks of constructing tents for Jesus, Moses and Elijah, employing the first person singular ('I will make') in place of Mark's plural verb ('let us make'). It is feasible that Peter has his own vocation in view – the vocation Jesus gives him at Caesarea Philippi – and imagines that the transfiguration offers him the opportunity to fulfil it, even in a small way, by constructing three tents to shelter the heavenly beings. He can begin to build that community (*ekklêsia*) in the here and now on the mount of transfiguration – thus, incidentally, bypassing the cross, a message that he has already struggled to grasp in the previous scene (16:21–3) and that Jesus will reinforce immediately following the transfiguration (17:12). Peter's mistake is an understandable one, therefore, in that he seeks to respond to his vocation as the foundation stone of the Christian community, without realizing that the Church can only be built on Jesus' obedience-unto-death.[40]

Unlike Mark's account, Peter's well-meaning but tenuous suggestion is interrupted in the next section by the cloud (17:5), which begins to enshroud the three heavenly beings even as Peter speaks ('while he was still speaking', 17:5a). This is the second time in the story that Matthew has employed the word 'behold'. The flimsy dwellings that Peter proposes erecting are paralleled by the intrusion of the divine cloud, which shelters the heavenly beings far more effectively than any human construction. The three are apparently obscured from the view of the disciples, who now have access only to the voice proceeding from the cloud (*ek*, meaning 'out of').[41] Matthew describes the cloud paradoxically as 'bright' (*phôteinê*, an adjective derived from the noun *phôs* meaning 'light'), strengthening the light symbolism of the story and underlining the presence of the *Shekinah*, the indwelling glory of God (see Ezek. 1:4; Apoc. 14:14). Just as Jesus' clothing radiates light and his face shines with the beauty of the sun, so the cloud shares the same heavenly radiance and beauty. Yet, whereas clouds normally obscure the light, this one is dazzling and full of light.

The parallel with Moses and the exodus is again plain. The same cloud – the pillar of cloud by day and pillar of fire by night – leads the children of Israel through the wilderness (Exod. 13:21–2; 40:36–8); it settles on Mount Sinai when Moses receives the law, embracing him as he ascends into the presence of God (Exod. 24:15–18; 34:5); it hovers over the tent of meeting where Moses speaks face to face with God (Num. 9:15–17) and over the mercy seat in the Holy of Holies (Lev. 16:2). Even in the Old Testament, while symbolic of the *Shekinah*, the cloud also indicates the awesome holiness of God which stands over against human beings, transcending human comprehension. The cloud reveals God's saving purposes, yet also veils the splendour of God, too bright for human eyes to gaze upon. Thus the cloud functions at two levels. On the one hand, it serves to conceal the mystery of Jesus' metamorphosis and the presence of his heavenly attendants from the uncomprehending gaze of the disciples. On the other hand, the cloud is revelatory, its brightness indicating celestial light, illuminating for the disciples the awesome presence of God as it descends upon Jesus and his heavenly companions.[42] The cloud 'simultaneously reveals and conceals the presence of God'.[43]

With the third use of 'behold' – coming so soon after the second – Matthew introduces the divine voice (17:5b). The words uttered are longer than in Mark's account, acclaiming Jesus not only as the beloved, but also as the well-pleasing Son (17:5; Mark 9:7). For Matthew, the epithet 'well-pleasing' (in verbal form, *eudokêsa*) expresses the Father's esteem for the chosen Son as he lives a life of submission to God, enacting that commitment to the law and its righteousness that Israel failed to achieve. The Old Testament background is probably the Servant of Isaiah (42:1) who is God's chosen one (which Matthew has already quoted at 12:18–21). There is thus a sense of recapitulation in Matthew's Gospel, a replaying of Israel's past which involves a radical self-emptying where the Son re-treads the path of the children of Israel and succeeds at the point where they foundered. For Matthew, Jesus is both 'God with us' (Emmanuel, 1:23) and the true Child of Israel whose humanity is fulfilled in his life of 'justice and mercy and faith' (23:23). Jesus is well-pleasing to God as Son in his divine origins and in his human life, where he reiterates Israel's history – its teaching and practice – bringing about salvation and throwing open Israel's election to the Gentiles.[44] The divine voice indicates that, in the transfiguration story, 'Israel's primal history is being recapitulated by her Messiah, God's Son, the eschatological embodiment of true Israel.'[45]

An important parallel at this point is Matthew's account of the baptism, which coheres closely with the transfiguration (3:13–17). We have already observed that, in Mark's account, the transfiguration is one of three moments of epiphany across the Gospel. There Jesus' identity as the divine Son is unveiled in palpable terms, each manifestation of divine glory intimately tied to the notion of suffering and powerlessness. Matthew shows greater interest in epiphanies than Mark, while making generous use of apocalyptic language and imagery. The coming of the Magi is an epiphany (2:1–12), with the light of the guiding star and the joy of finding the infant with his mother, Mary (2:11). The baptism is likewise an epiphany where the Spirit descends like a dove and the divine voice acclaims Jesus' identity (3:13–17), more publicly than in the Markan account. Through the dialogue with John the Baptist, Matthew shows that the epiphany of the baptism – Jesus' descent into the water – represents a fulfilling of 'all righteousness', the living out of the law, in word and deed, by which Jesus enacts that love and loyalty which is Israel's side of the covenant. Matthew's language is less forceful than Mark's. The heavens 'open' upon Jesus' ascent from the water, while the Spirit descends and the voice of God speaks, and it is clear that the heavens open so that the Spirit may come and the voice proclaim (3:16–17). God speaks in identical wording at the baptism and the transfiguration, using the third person in both scenes ('This is ...'), rather than the second person, 'you', as in Mark's account of the baptism. In this way Matthew binds together, as closely as possible, the baptism and transfiguration.

Other incidents in Matthew partake of the same character as epiphany. Jesus' appearance on the water and the disciples' recognition have a similar quality (14:22–33), as does Peter's declaration at Caesarea Philippi (16:13–20). On the cross, the events are more spectacular than in Mark and suggest that it becomes ironically an epiphany. In the mockery (27:40, 43) Jesus is tested for his commitment to God, with all its implications for enduring the cross and remaining faithful and obedient, even in God's absence (27:46).[46] It is not the desolation of Jesus' death that affects the Roman soldiers, as with the centurion in Mark's account, but the apocalyptic events surrounding the crucifixion which, in Matthew, are more manifold and dramatic. Indeed, the resurrection itself intrudes, as it were, into the crucifixion, as if it can no longer hold itself back. At the point of Jesus' death, after the tearing of the temple veil,[47] the earthquake that splits open the tombs causes the righteous to rise from their graves and appear in Jerusalem (27:51–3). Jesus' death, for Matthew, is an event that shakes the earth to its foundations: 'While the bystanders look on unmoved, mocking and uncertain, the very rocks reel and shatter.'[48] When the Son of God dies in compliance to the Father's will, forsaking all things (including the divine presence) and displaying perfect trust in 'every word that proceeds from the mouth of God' (4:4), the earth, the Underworld, even death itself, open to the sovereign power of God.

Finally, at the end of the Gospel, the resurrection too has the form and features of an epiphany. The two women disciples receive unexpectedly an appearance of the risen Christ, worship him and obey his directives, without a trace of the ambiguity we find in Mark (Matthew 28:1–10; Mark 16:8). Later, on the mountain, Jesus displays the glory of his sovereignty to the eleven, not only because he is Son of God in status and nature (from his conception), but because he has obediently traversed the paths of life and death, descending into the deepest darkness of God's absence, and opening the cosmic levels to divine authority (28:18).

Throughout Matthew's Gospel, the title 'Son of God' is surprisingly frequent, in comparison to Mark. Twice already the disciples, responding to revelation from above, have declared their conviction that Jesus is the divine Son (14:33; 16:16), both incidents showing, as we have seen, the characteristics of an epiphany.[49] The title is a major one in Matthew – indeed, may well be the most important in this Gospel.[50] Although in the Old Testament 'son of God' refers to the role of the king in Israel, in Matthew's hand, it takes on weightier connotations;[51] here Matthew is influenced by Mark, although he develops the title in his own way. Jesus is not only son of David and son of Abraham (1:1), not only son of Mary by birth and of Joseph by adoption (1:16), he is also Son of God through his virginal conception, revealed explicitly in Matthew's third Old Testament quotation in the birth narrative: 'out of Egypt have I called my son' (2:15;

Jer. 31:5). The same theme is divulged by the voice at the baptism (3:17) and confirmed in the temptation narrative where Jesus vindicates his status as the divine Son through his perfect trust in the Father (4:3, 6).

The metamorphosis and all its imagery – the illumination of Jesus' body and clothing, the attendant figures of Moses and Elijah, the shining cloud and the voice – all declare symbolically the one message and proclaim the one identity: that Jesus is the beloved, unique, well-pleasing Son of the Father, 'revealed in his essential divine glory'.[52] At the transfiguration, Jesus' divine sonship eclipses even Matthew's own stress on the superiority of Jesus to Moses.[53] The theme of light and brightness associated with Jesus – in his person and in the cloud – is 'a figurative representation of his intimate relationship with the Father'.[54] The title is the same as Peter's confession at Caesarea Philippi, confirming not just the message of the cross but more fundamentally Jesus' identity, an identity that even for Peter is the result of divine revelation rather than human reasoning or insight. 'Son of God' encompasses Jesus in his suffering and glory, his illuminated presence on the mountain peak and his surrender to God that will take him the weary, painful path of the cross. It is present at Gethsemane which is 'almost a parody of the transfiguration',[55] concerned with the 'testing of Jesus' filial obedience' of the Father and displaying the inner meaning of the cross, by which sins will be forgiven.[56] Matthew's use of 'Son of God' encompasses Jesus' entire ministry – his life and death – which is understood as the playing out of a divinely-ordained vocation.

Yet the transfiguration is not concerned primarily with Jesus' filial conformity to the divine will, unless we think its sole function is to confirm Jesus' message of the cross in the previous scene. If we are to give the title its full weight at the transfiguration, we need to set it alongside Peter's confession of faith, 'You are the Christ, the Son of the living God', a confession that earns Peter a beatitude: 'Blessed are you, Simon, son of John, for flesh and blood has not revealed this to you but my Father who is in heaven' (16:16–17). In each case, there is recognition of the other as 'son', though Jesus' sonship far exceeds that of Peter, son of John; here Jesus is not 'son of Joseph' but 'Son of God'. Joseph's adoptive fatherhood goes only a limited way to repairing the tear in the genealogy when the procession of male begettings suddenly halts at the critical moment, just before the end. Jesus is not begotten of Joseph but 'born of Mary' (1:16),[57] the Holy Spirit being the ultimate source of his life (1:20). Jesus' identity, both here and at the transfiguration, is divinely given and divinely revealed, not humanly surmised even on the basis of the Old Testament. While Jesus forges an obedience for Israel through life and death, therefore, his sonship expresses his status from the beginning. The resurrection is the vindication of that sonship and authority which, though in one sense possessing all along, he replays in his righteous life and reclaims in the resurrection, on the basis of the salvation he has wrought.[58] In the same way, the voice at the transfiguration is 'a vindication of Jesus' refusal to accept a truncated kingly sovereignty and a premature glory at the cost of his fundamental identity as the glorious Son of the Father who is in heaven'.[59] Jesus both is and becomes Son of God in this Gospel; he possesses divine authority from the beginning yet also in another sense gains it; he is gifted with the title before his birth, foretold in the story of Israel (2:15), yet earns it by his obedient life and death.

There is an important Matthæan parallel to the language of revelation and sonship at 11:25–7. There Jesus, in the guise of Wisdom, addresses God as 'Father' and speaks of divine revelation being given, not to the wise and knowing, but to infants (11:25). This theological insight is described as 'well-pleasing' to God (*eudokêsa*, 11:26, the same verb used at 17:5). What follows is an extraordinary statement of Jesus' relationship with God in Father–Son language that may seem more reminiscent of John's Gospel but is nonetheless at home in Matthew: 'All things have been handed over to me by my Father, and no-one knows the Son except the Father, nor does anyone know the Father except the Son and the one to whom the Son chooses to reveal him' (11:27). The language articulates a unique relationship grounded in intimacy, sovereignty and oneness of purpose. At both Caesarea Philippi and on the mount of transfiguration, the disciples are the infants to whom revelation has been given, and the core of that revelation is Jesus as the unique Son of the Father to whom 'all things' have been handed over. In Matthew, there is an equally strong sense of God in relation to disciples as 'your Father',[60] or 'our Father' in the Lord's Prayer (6:9);[61] but Jesus' use of 'my Father' is singular and, while overlapping, is distinct from that of disciples' relationship with God.[62] The distinction is symbolized in the virginal conception, where Jesus' birth both parallels and differs from ordinary human birth. It is visible throughout Jesus' ministry in his intimate knowledge of God, and his possession of divine authority.

It could be argued that, in Matthew, the divine voice plays a more important role than in Mark and that the meaning of the transfiguration is to be found mainly in God's speech, emanating from the cloud.[63] The disciples, after all, respond by falling down only after hearing the voice. As

with Mark's account, however, this is a reductionist reading of the story:
the disciples 'did not fall down because of the voice, since this had happened frequently before ... but ... because of this wonderful and extraordinary light'.[64] The disciples, as we have observed, already know Jesus'
identity as the Son of God, the voice at the baptism being public rather
than private, and they have already acclaimed him Son of God (14:33). The
function of the voice at the transfiguration is rather to explain and interpret the metamorphosis to them, and indeed the whole event, including
the symbolic presence of Moses and Elijah. The disciples' fear is as much
a response to the luminous cloud as to the voice, and most probably arises
from the whole transfiguration, from beginning to end. The function of the
voice is thus not informative, in the sense of communicating (as in Mark)
new information to the disciples. Its revelatory function is to confirm the
disciples' apprehension of Jesus on the water, and Peter's confession at
Caesarea Philippi (16:16), particularly in the light of the founding of the
Church and Jesus' revelation of his forthcoming suffering, death and
resurrection. The Gospel gives the disciples a tangible experience of the
majesty of the Son of God, a majesty already visible in his infancy, but yet
to be confirmed in his resurrection appearance on the mountain in Galilee.
It is not just the hearing but the hearing in relation to the seeing ('vision',
17:9). The metamorphosis is the visible manifestation of Jesus as Son and
therefore Lord of the Church, represented here by the three disciples, one
of them already named the Rock.[65]

As in Mark, the voice of the Father also enjoins the disciples to 'listen
to him', a word that, especially in Matthew, implies obedience as well as
hearing. These words are not part of the baptismal epiphany.[66] For Mark,
this instruction relates specifically to the passion and resurrection predictions on the journey to Jerusalem, where Jesus discloses the necessity of
his suffering. While the same message is present in Matthew's account,
the focus is broader.[67] The reference to a prophet-like-Moses underlies
Matthew's Gospel (Deut. 18:15), with its discourses and its focus on Jesus
as the one who teaches the will of God and authenticates that teaching in
his life. The one who interprets the eternal law of Moses (5:17–18) with
the words, 'but I say to you' (5:22, 28, 32, 34, 39, 44), is the one who has
already overcome the devil with his authoritative word, has healed the
sick, has called disciples to take on his 'easy yoke' (11:28–30), and has
revealed the mysteries of the kingdom of heaven (13:11); in future chapters he will give instructions for the life of the Church, and pronounce
God's apocalyptic salvation and judgement on the nations as Son of Man

and Judge (23–5).[68] Thus God's mandate at the transfiguration will become that of Jesus after the resurrection, fulfilled because of his perpetual presence with the disciples (28:16–20).[69] The divine confirmation of Jesus' teaching – a teaching vindicated in his life and work – is addressed to the three disciples as representatives of the newly constituted community. The Church proclaims Jesus as the divine Son whose teaching has its source in God, whose eternal presence embraces the Old Testament witness, and whose 'utterances have a final and incomparable authority'.[70]

Matthew gives heightened emphasis to the disciples' response to the bright cloud and the voice, indicating that the transfiguration is for their benefit and ultimately their transfiguration (17:6). The disciples respond in an appropriate fashion to an epiphany or an apocalyptic vision (see Dan. 10:8–12):[71] they are overcome by fear and fall on their faces. As in Mark, the fear is fundamentally the awe and terror evoked by divine reality, manifest in sight and sound, a reality that transcends the created world. In falling down, however, the disciples are also in an attitude suggestive of worship.[72] At the beginning and end of Matthew, we find the same motif: the Magi fall down and worship the infant (2:11); the two women disciples at the empty tomb fall at Jesus' feet in worship (28:9). In both cases, these seemingly unlikely people (Gentiles and women) show their capacity to see, hear and obey the signs of divine presence. Epiphanies characteristically give rise to holy fear and prostration, and Matthew follows the same tradition. Like the two females at the empty tomb, the three male disciples symbolize the Church and respond with awe and worship, overcome by the dread of whom they see and what they hear. The majestic presence of Christ shines forth with a burning light that overwhelms them and fills them with holy awe.

Matthew's Jesus does not leave the disciples overwhelmed by his glory but comes forward to reassure and comfort them: fear and love go together (17:7). Matthew expresses this reassurance in three ways (17:7). First, Jesus actively *approaches* the disciples (*prosêlthen*) as they lie on the ground. The verb 'approach' is used throughout the Gospel in virtually a cultic sense and refers to those who make formal application to Jesus for supplication, instruction or worship.[73] Yet here the roles are reversed: now it is Jesus who makes formal approach to the disciples. The only other time in which Jesus approaches his disciples is on the mountain in Galilee after the resurrection (28:18), a parallel that forges, as we have already seen, close links with the transfiguration. On both occasions, the context is the revelation of Christ's divine, life-giving glory, where he stands before them in 'an exalted state'.[74] This motif articulates symbolically the advent of God's salvation. As Emmanuel, God-with-us, Jesus approaches, first Israel, then the Gentiles (see 15:21–8), with compassion and authority, offering reassurance and life.

Second, Jesus not only approaches the disciples but also *touches* them (*hapsamenos*). Jesus' touch elsewhere in the Gospel is for the purpose of healing, its power extending to his clothing (8:3, 15; 9:20, 29; 14:36; 20:34). Always it is a compassionate, saving touch that brings health and wholeness to those who experience it. The transfiguration is the only place where it does not have the literal sense of healing, but rather means comforting, reassuring and giving life. It also communicates a sense of intimacy, conveying love and understanding in the midst of fear, and drawing close those whom awe and terror have pushed away.

Third, Jesus instructs the disciples to *rise*, using a word charged with theological and symbolic meaning (*egerthête*). Twice in the immediate surrounding context the same verb, in the passive voice, is used of Jesus' resurrection from the dead (*egerthênai*, 16:21; *egerthê[i]*, 17:9; see 9:25). Although Jesus at one level is simply raising the terrified disciples to their feet, at another level he is raising them to a new life, anticipating the end time (see 26:46).[75] Jesus calls them to participate in his own metamorphosis where, like him, they will one day 'shine like the sun in the kingdom of their Father' (13:43). By approach, by touch and by word of life, Jesus thus reassures and comforts his disciples, setting alongside his terrifying majesty an intimacy of love and understanding.

When the overcome disciples, strengthened by Jesus, are finally able to raise their eyes, they *see* only Jesus, no longer transfigured (17:8). The departure of Moses and Elijah stresses, even more strongly than in Mark, that their role is now replaced by Jesus himself. This is particularly telling, given the stress Matthew places on Moses. The disciples thus receive insight into Jesus' unique identity and future destiny, though first they must accompany him to Jerusalem. There will be no overt glory and no radiance on this hard path, but the sight and the hearing will sustain them. They will learn that the glorious Son of God is also the obedient Son, and that their salvation depends on his capacity to ascend the Mount of Olives, just as he ascended the mount of transfiguration. Only then can the mount of commissioning be reached, when his eternal presence will be promised them – the final reassurance – so strengthening them to continue his mercy and mission.

Yet the revelation witnessed by these three representatives of the Church is not yet for the telling. Only in the light of the resurrection can the story be told (17:9). In Matthew the meaning is specific: Jesus must first commission the eleven disciples on the mountain, once his authority is made public through his obedient death on the cross and his victory over death. The vision on the mount of transfiguration must be complemented by the appearance of the risen Christ on the mount of commissioning. In between these two mountains, the valley of the shadow of death must first be traversed, each moment on the journey – whether valley or mountain – revealing the same paradoxical truth of Jesus' identity as the glorious, yet obedient, Son. The three disciples may for the moment be deprived of glory and condemned to silence, but the inability to speak about what they have seen and heard – like their experience of the glory – is only temporary: the resurrection and beyond that the parousia will make that splendour no longer hidden or occasional. The one who remains alone with them now, after the brightness has faded, after Moses and Elijah have vanished and the bright cloud drifted away, will remain with them always, through suffering and tribulation, to 'the end of the age' (28:20; see 18:20).

Matthew's form of the transfiguration story has a dual focus, concerned equally with Jesus and the disciples. Jesus is the beloved Son whose true identity is disclosed to the eyes of faith, the foundation of the Church's life and teaching. Jesus' divine sonship is attested to throughout Matthew's Gospel: in his birth, his ministry, his death and resurrection, and, at the centre of the Gospel, his transfiguration. Both the glory of the mountain peak and the degradation and agony of the cross reveal his sonship, divine and human, evinced in a life of righteousness in which he chooses 'not the Satanic way of world dominance but the way of obedience laid out for him by God'.[76] While his identity is manifest on the mount of transfiguration only to the three, its full radiance and beauty will shine forth on the mount of commissioning, where Jesus once more will approach his fearful, doubting disciples, giving them his authority to proclaim his teaching to 'all the nations'. On the mount of transfiguration, he re-enacts the story of Moses' ascent up Mount Sinai, revealing himself as the one who embodies the law in word and deed. As the transfigured Son of God, Jesus not only appears to his Church but draws them into his life-giving resurrection power, lifting them, as he does also at Gethsemane, into the divine life that he shares with the Father. Jesus' metamorphosis is thus a powerful symbol in Matthew of Jesus' identity, an identity that brings into being the Church which is founded in his name and anticipates God's glorious future.[77]

Notes

1 Davies, W. D. and Allison, D. C., *A Critical and Exegetical Commentary on the Gospel According to Saint Matthew*, 3 vols (ed. J. A. Emerton et al.), T. & T. Clark, Edinburgh, 1988–97, 627.

2 Luz, U., *Matthew 8–20: A Commentary* (trans. J. E. Crouch, ed. H. Koester), Fortress, Minneapolis, MN, 2001, 401, 403.

3 Moses, A. D. A., *Matthew's Transfiguration Story and Jewish–Christian Controversy* (ed. S. E. Porter), Sheffield Academic Press, Sheffield, 1996, 91.

4 Harrington, D. J., *The Gospel of Matthew*, Liturgical Press, Collegeville, MN, 1991, 255.

5 Luz, *op. cit.*, 395–7.

6 Davies and Allison, *op. cit.*, 684, see a chiasm here, with the voice at the centre; also Luz, *op. cit.*, 394.

7 Hagner, D. A., *Matthew 14–28*, vol. 2, Word Books, Dallas, TX, 1995, 491–2, and Boring, M. E., 'Matthew', in *The New Interpreter's Bible*, Abingdon, Nashville, TN, 1995, 8, 364.

8 W. Michaelis, '*Horama*', in Kittel, G. (ed.), *Theological Dictionary of the New Testament*, vol. 5, Eerdmans, Grand Rapids, MI, 1967, 371–2.

9 Davies and Allison, *op. cit.*, 685–8, see Moses as the key to the transfiguration rather than the apocalyptic imagery; also Allison, D. C., *The New Moses: A Matthean Typology*, Fortress, Minneapolis, MN, 1993, 243–8; see Gundry, R. H., *Matthew: A Commentary on his Handbook for a Mixed Church under Persecution*, 2nd edn, Eerdmans, Grand Rapids, MI, 1994, 342–6. For Moses, op. cit., 50–113, the story is a synthesis of Moses–Sinai and apocalyptic traditions.

10 These are: the Sermon on the Mount (Matt. 5–7), the Missionary Discourse (Matt. 10), the Parables (Matt. 13), the Community Rules (Matt. 18) and the Apocalyptic Discourse (Matt. 24–5).

11 Davies and Allison, *op. cit.*, 693–4.

12 The order is different, with Andrew's name between Peter and the sons of Zebedee (10:2).

13 The addition of 'brother' suggests the community of disciples (cf. 18:15, 21, 35); so Gundry, *op. cit.*, 342, and Boring, *op. cit.*, 363.

14 After the third prediction, it is the mother of James and John who requests seats in the kingdom for her sons (20:20–3).

15 See Donaldson, T. L., *Jesus on the Mountain: A Study in Matthean Theology*, JSOT Press, Sheffield, 1985, especially pp. vi–vii.

16 Luz, *op. cit.*, 398.

17 Bornkamm, G., 'The Stilling of the Storm in Matthew', in Bornkamm, G., Barth, G. and Held, H. J. (eds), *Traditional Interpretation in Matthew*, SCM, London, 1963, 52–7.

18 For this distinction, relevant to the structure of Matthew 5–11, see Schweizer, E., *The Good News According to Matthew: A Commentary on the Gospel* (trans. D. E. Green), SPCK, London, 1975, 69–74.

19 On the links between the two scenes, see Kenny, A., 'The Transfiguration and the Agony in the Garden', *Catholic Biblical Quarterly* 19, 1957, 445–8.

20 Luz, *op. cit.*, 399.

21 The points of agreement between Matthew and Luke against Mark are the reference to Jesus' face and the cloud interrupting Peter – probably coincidental; see Neirynck, F., 'Minor Agreements Matthew–Luke in the Transfiguration Story', in Hoffmann, P. (ed.), *Orientierung an Jesus: Zur Theologie der Synoptiker*, Herder, Freiburg, 1973, 253–65.

22 In Philo, *The Life of Moses* (trans. F. H. Colson) (Loeb Classical Library, vol. 6 of 12), Harvard University Press, Cambridge, MA, 1984, II.70, Moses' face flashes rays like the sun; see Davies and Allison, *op. cit.*, 696.

23 See Philo's use of ascent and transfiguration language for Moses (Philo, *Moses*, I.57, 158–9; II.288–9; Philo, *Questions and Answers on Exodus* (trans. R. Marcus) (vol. Supplement II of 12), Harvard University Press, Cambridge, MA, 1987, 2.29; Moses, *op. cit.*, 52–4.

24 Kingsbury, J. D., *Matthew: Structure, Christology, Kingdom*, Fortress Press, Philadelphia, 1975, 68; also Moses, *op. cit.*, 122.

25 E.g. 2 Enoch 1:5; 2 Baruch 51:3; 4 Ezra 7:97; also 1 Enoch 14:21; Apoc. 1:16.

26 Gregory Palamas, *Homily 34*, in McGuckin, J. A., *The Transfiguration of Christ in Scripture and Tradition*, Edwin Mellen, Lewiston, NY, 1986, 232.

27 Viviano, B. T., 'The Gospel According to Matthew', in Brown, R. E. et al. (eds), *The New Jerome Biblical Commentary*, Geoffrey Chapman, London, 1990, 660.

28 See, e.g., Philo, *Questions on Genesis*, I.86.

29 Gregory of Nyssa, *Life of Moses*, connects the light of the burning bush with the light of the transfiguration; see Nes, S., *The Uncreated Light: An Iconographical Study of the Transfiguration in the Eastern Church*, Eastern Christian Publications, Fairfax, VA, 2002, 98–100.

30 Davies and Allison, *op. cit.*, 687; also Moses, *op. cit.*, 191.

31 Allison, *op. cit.*, 271–90.

32 Donaldson, *op. cit.*, 148.

33 Moses, *op. cit.*, 131. Judas Iscariot calls Jesus 'Rabbi' at the arrest at Gethsemane (26:25).

34 Heil, J. P., *The Transfiguration of Jesus: Narrative Meaning and Function of Mark 9:2–8, Matt 17:1–8 and Luke 9:28–36*, Editrice Pontificio Istituto Biblico, Rome, 2000, 115–27, lists the possibilities; Davies and Allison, *op. cit.*, 699–700, are undecided.

35 See, e.g., Boobyer, G. H., *St. Mark and the Transfiguration Story*, T. & T. Clark, Edinburgh, 1942, 76–9, Riesenfeld, H., *Jésus Transfiguré: L'arrière-plan du récit Évangélique de la Transfiguration de Notre-Seigneur*, Munksgaard, Copenhagen, 1947, 265–80, Beare, F. W., *The Gospel According to Matthew*, Blackwell, Oxford, 1981, 364, and Viviano, *op. cit.*, 660.

36 Stock, A., *The Method and Message of Matthew*, Liturgical Press, Collegeville, MN, 1994, 275–6, and Hagner, *op. cit.*, 493–4.

37 1 Enoch 39:3–8; Testament of Abraham A 20:13–14; Schweizer, *Matthew*, 348–9.

38 Harrington, *Matthew*, 254.

39 Senior, D. *Matthew* (Nashville, TN: Abingdon, 1998) p. 197.

40 Moses, *op. cit.*, 131–2.

41 Against this, cf. Stock, *op. cit.*, 276.

42 For Heil, *op. cit.*, 143–8, and Davies and Allison, *op. cit.*, 701, 704, the cloud acts as a vehicle for Moses and Elijah – if so, it is strange that they do not arrive on one.

43 Schweizer, *Matthew*, 349.

44 Against this, a minority see Matthew as remaining within Judaism; e.g. Sim, D. C., *The Gospel of Matthew and Christian Judaism: The History and Social Setting of the Matthean Community* (ed. John Barclay et al.), T. & T. Clark, Edinburgh, 1998, 109–63.

45 Davies and Allison, *op. cit.*, 705.

46 *Ibid.*, 706–7, contrast the transfiguration as a private epiphany, full of light, flanked by 'two religious giants from the past', with the crucifixion as a public spectacle, full of darkness, flanked by 'two common, convicted criminals'. In both Jesus is the Son of God.

47 Stock, *op. cit.*, 428–9, argues that Matthew's reader know the veil is a tapestry depicting the heavens; also Schmidt, T. E., 'The Penetration of Barriers and the Revelation of Christ in the Gospels', *Novum Testamentum* 34, 1992, 229–30.

48 Schweizer, *Matthew*, 515.

49 Kingsbury, *Matthew: Structure*, 58–60.

50 *Ibid.*, 40–83, and Moses, *op. cit.*, 195–201. Kingsbury sees the title as a confession of faith, inaccessible to non-believers (57, 82–3).

51 Kingsbury, *Matthew: Structure*, 47, 78–83. The background is most likely Psalm 2:7, though there may also be an allusion to Isaac (Gen. 22); so McCurley, F. R., '"and after Six Days" (Mark 9:2): A Semitic Literary Device', *Journal of Biblical Literature* 93, 1974, 78–80. For enthronement overtones, see Donaldson, *op. cit.*, 146–8, 151–6; also Riesenfeld, *op. cit.*, 223–35, 265–80.

52 Beare, *op. cit.*, 361; also Gundry, *op. cit.*, 344–5.

53 Barton, S. C., 'The Transfiguration of Christ According to Mark and Matthew: Christology and Anthropology', in Avemarie, F. and Lichtenberger, H. (eds), *Auferstehung – Resurrection*, J. C. B. Mohr (Paul Siebeck), Tübingen, 2001, 241.

54 Patte, D., *The Gospel According to Matthew: A Structural Commentary on Matthew's Faith*, Fortress, Philadelphia, 1987, 237.

55 Barton, '*Auferstehung*', 242.

56 *Ibid.*, 242–3.

57 The verb *gennân* refers in the active to the male role and in the passive to the female (1:2–16).

58 The same paradox is found in Hebrews, where Jesus is the eternal Son, above all created things (Heb. 1:1–4), and the one who earns sonship through suffering and obedience (Heb. 5:5–10).

59 Barton, '*Auferstehung*', 242.

60 E.g. Matt. 5:16; 6:1, 14, 26; 7:11; 10:20; 18:14; 23:9.

61 On God's fatherhood in relation to disciples, see Barton, S. C., *The Spirituality of the Gospels*, SPCK, London, 1992, 12–14.

62 Thompson, M. M., *The Promise of the Father: Jesus and God in the New Testament*, Westminster/John Knox, Louisville, KY, 2000, 105–14. See Matt. 6:4; 7:21; 10:32–3; 12:50; 15:13; 18:10; 25:34; 26:39, 42.

63 Heil, *op. cit.*, 216, Davies and Allison, *op. cit.*, 703, Beare, *op. cit.*, 365, and Luz, *op. cit.*, 394.

64 Gregory Palamas, *Homily* 35, in McGuckin, *op. cit.*, 235.

65 Moses, *op. cit.*, 145, 159.

66 Heil, *op. cit.*, 216, argues that it is the mandate which overwhelms the disciples, not the declaration of Jesus as Son which does not affect them at the baptism. Yet Jesus is not metamorphosed there and in

Matthew the commands to listen do not overwhelm them (5:21–48; 7:24; 11:15; 13:9, 43; 15:10).

67 Gundry, *op. cit.*, 345.

68 The difficult title 'Son of Man' in Matthew is probably eschatological (Dan. 7:13–14), showing Jesus as the world's Judge; Kingsbury, *Matthew: Structure*, 113–22, and Moses, *op. cit.*, 85–113.

69 Heil, *op. cit.*, 252–3.

70 Hagner, *op. cit.*, 495.

71 Patte, *op. cit.*, 237–8, regards it as inappropriate: a turning away from heaven.

72 Gundry, *op. cit.*, 345, and Hagner, *op. cit.*, 494.

73 See Matt. 5:1; 8:2, 5, 19, 25; 9:14, 20, 28; 13:10, 36; 14:14; 15:12, 23, 30; 17:14, 19; 18:1, 21; 19:16; 20:20; 21:14; 24:1; 26:7, 17; 28:9. Jesus is also approached by his enemies (e.g. 16:1; 19:3; 22:23) and poignantly by Judas with a kiss (26:49); angels and the devil also 'approach' him (4:3, 11; see 28:2).

74 Davies and Allison, *op. cit.*, 703.

75 Schweizer, *Matthew*, 349–40.

76 Luz, *op. cit.*, 398.

77 Matthew's perspective is essentially theocentric; so Boring, *op. cit.*, 353–61.

3
The Transfiguration in Luke

9:28 It happened after these words, about eight days later, that taking Peter, John and James he ascended the mountain to pray. 29 And it happened while he was praying that the appearance of his face became different and his clothing became dazzling white. 30 And behold two men were talking together with him, who were, Moses and Elijah, 31 who having appeared in glory were speaking about his departure which he was about to fulfil in Jerusalem. 32 Now Peter and those with him were heavy with sleep; but when they were fully awake they saw his glory and the two men who were standing with him. 33 And it happened that while they were separating from him Peter said to Jesus, 'Master, it is good for us to be here; so let us make three tents, one for you, one for Moses and one for Elijah' – not knowing what he was saying. 34 And while he was saying these things a cloud came and overshadowed them; and they were afraid as they entered into the cloud. 35 And a voice came from the cloud, saying: 'This is my chosen Son; to him listen .' 36 And when the voice had spoken, Jesus was found alone. And they themselves were silent and reported to no-one in those days anything of what they had seen. 37 And it happened on the next day, when they had come down from the mountain, that a large crowd came to meet him.

(Luke 9:27–37)

The story of the transfiguration in the Gospel of Luke is a vivid account of Jesus' experience on the mountain while in the context of prayer. Jesus' radiance, the presence of Moses and Elijah, the glory that surrounds them, the conversation between them and the destiny that faces him, are all symbolic of the divine visitation which is the centre of Luke's theology. In contrast, the three disciples fail to grasp what is happening around them, their insight impeded by drowsiness, misunderstanding and fear. Yet the disciples are portrayed as sympathetic characters: their inadequacy in the face of the glory is comprehensible. The solitude of Jesus and the silence of his disciples at the end stand in contrast to the transfiguration itself, with its luminescence, fellowship and solemn speech. Theologically, the

Lukan transfiguration empowers Jesus to confront his fate through
prayer, leading his disciples on the journey of death to life, a grim journey
that will finally embrace them with glory.

The transfiguration occurs at the centre of Luke's Gospel, closely
bound to what precedes and follows it.[1] It is tied to the revelation of Jesus'
suffering and death, showing the divine glory in the context of the passion.
The story functions as the climax to the Galilean ministry (4:14–9:50), and
points forward to the journey Jesus will undertake to Jerusalem, the
centre of salvation-history (9:51–19:28). Luke connects the transfiguration
both to Galilee and Jerusalem, the two major phases of Jesus' ministry in
this Gospel. Luke's transfiguration is an epiphany,[2] disclosing Jesus in his
glory as the Son and Chosen One of the Father. At one level, Luke's version of the transfiguration follows Mark's account: the ascent up the
mountain, the events of the transfiguration, including the disciples' misunderstanding, and the descent down the mountain at the end. However,
Luke also agrees with Matthew over against Mark in at least two important respects: the reference to Jesus' face and the arrival of the cloud while
Peter is speaking – agreements that are most likely coincidental.[3] Yet
Luke's story is different from either Mark or Matthew; apart from anything else, it is significantly longer.

So divergent is the Lukan account that, in the judgement of some, Luke
has obtained access to another version of the transfiguration which he has
wedded to the Markan story.[4] Unique to Luke are the context of Jesus'
prayer, the reference to glory, the discussion concerning Jesus' departure,
the lassitude of the disciples, the voice naming Jesus as 'chosen', and the
absence of conversation between Jesus and the disciples on their descent
down the mountain. A second source, in addition to Mark, would certainly explain many of these variations, though it is important not to underestimate the extent of Luke's own creative editing.[5] Though it is most likely that the changes are Luke's own, there remains the possibility that
Luke has had access to a second source. In either event, Luke has cre-
atively re-worked the transfiguration story – whether from one or more
sources – to develop his own tale, with its own characteristic emphases.

Luke's story of the transfiguration belongs within a wider narrative
frame concerned with the question of Jesus' identity (9:1–50). The question is posed by Herod – 'Who is this of whom I hear such things?' (9:9) –
and answered in the ensuing episodes which together form the central section of Luke's Gospel. Each scene answers the question in a different way,
preparing the reader for the journey to Jerusalem. The question of his

identity is reiterated by Jesus himself, for the crowds and for the disciples (presumably the twelve).[6] In comparison to Mark, Luke compresses Peter's confession of faith and the revelation of the way of the cross, so that they become one scene (9:18–27) in which Peter's succinct confession – 'You are the Christ of God' – leads directly to Jesus' prediction of his passion, death and resurrection. His discourse on the way of the cross climaxes in the coming of the Son of Man in glory. Not long after the descent from the mount of transfiguration – which overlaps with the next story (9:37) – Luke announces in portentous language the commencement of the journey to Jerusalem, 'the city of destiny' (9:51).[7] Jesus sets his face towards the city that is the goal of Luke–Acts, the centre of salvation history, from whence the gospel will fan out 'to the ends of the earth' (Acts 1:8).

There is a circular pattern to the whole section. The two central scenes concern suffering and glory (9:18–27, 28–36), the way of the cross and the transfiguration, and are joined by the saying about God's reign or kingdom (*basileia*, 9:27) which concludes the first scene and moves towards the second. Significantly, unlike Mark, these two innermost scenes find Jesus at prayer. Two miracles – feeding and exorcism – match each other, underlining the theme of Jesus' compassionate and liberating ministry and also the importance of the miraculous, in Luke's understanding, as an incentive to faith (9:10–17, 37–43a). Herod's curiosity, behind which lurk his anxiety and enmity, parallels Jesus' second reference to the passion and resurrection, where he predicts that he will be 'betrayed into human hands' (9:7–9, 43b–8). The frame shows the potential ability yet misunderstanding of the twelve in regard to ministry and mission (9:1–6, 49–50): see Table 3.1.

Table 3.1

a Mission and ministry of 12 (9:1–6)	**a¹** Disciples prevent ministry of unknown exorcist (9:49–50)
b Herod, Jesus' enemy, asks question of his identity (9:7–9)	**b¹** Jesus handed over to his enemies and misunderstood by disciples (9:43b–48)
c Jesus' ministry: power to feed hungry (9:10–17)	**c¹** Jesus' ministry: power over demons (9:37–43a)
d Jesus at prayer: way of cross (9:18–27) *Jesus is dying and rising Messiah and Son of Man who will come in glory*	**d¹** Jesus at prayer: transfiguration (9:28–36) *Jesus is Son of Father, God's Chosen One*

Although Luke retains Mark's three passion and resurrection predictions, they are not as dominant nor so evenly distributed.[8] Luke particularly emphasizes the passion in the lead-up to 9:51. Throughout the journey, a major motif is that of the journey itself, as the homeless Son of Man wends his way to the holy city.[9]

Luke's transfiguration story falls easily into two parts. The first concerns Jesus' own experience (9:28–31): the change in his appearance, the presence of Moses and Elijah and the all-important subject of their conversation, while the second deals with the experience of the disciples: their somnolence, Peter's suggestion, their fear and silence (9:32–6).[10] The ascent and descent of the mountain form a loose frame, although the descent is narrated as the beginning of the next story (Table 3.2).

Table 3.2

Ascent *(9:28)*	
Jesus ascends the mountain to pray in	
company with three disciples	
Jesus' transfiguration *(9:29–31)*	• Change in Jesus' appearance (9:29)
	• Conversation with Moses and Elijah
	about his departure in Jerusalem (9:30–1)
Disciples' response *(9:32–6)*	• Disciples heavy with sleep (9:32)
	• Peter's suggestion of three tents (9:33)
	• Intervening cloud and disciples' fear (9:34)
	• Voice from cloud, disappearance of signs and
	disciples' silence (9:35)
Descent *(9:37)*	
Jesus and his disciples descend the	
mountain the next day	

This structure is not the same as Mark's and indicates that Luke's story is considerably different, even while incorporating much of the same symbolism. The interpretation and meaning of the transfiguration are hard to separate from the literary structure. Here, as elsewhere, form and content belong together.

Luke begins his story of the transfiguration by connecting it with Jesus' discourse on the way of the cross (9:28–9).[11] The transfiguration is a new scene ('and it happened'), but it follows immediately from Jesus' prophecy that some of those present will not die until they see God's reign (9:27). Luke's language is briefer and less ambiguous than Mark's: 'until they see the reign (kingdom) of God' (9:27; Mark 9:1). Whereas for Mark the implications are that God's reign is still to come – however confusing – Luke is more straightforward. He is speaking of the transfiguration itself, which will be a true manifestation of the reign of God for the disciples, even if not its final advent. Jesus' message of taking up the cross as the chief characteristic and challenge of discipleship – and on a daily basis (9:23) – follows from his own death, just as the life which the disciples experience is dependent on his resurrection and parousia (9:24–6). Death and glory are themes that run explicitly through both scenes, binding them together even more closely, if possible, than in Mark.

The time reference between the two closely connected events – the way of the cross and the transfiguration – is 'about eight days', according to Luke (9:28). In inclusive counting, this means a week (see John 20:26). Luke disregards Mark's calculation of six days, with its overtones of Moses on Mount Sinai, and rounds the number to a week, making it smoother and less abrupt than Mark's reckoning.[12] Luke also smoothes out Mark's wording of the ascent up the mountain: Jesus does not 'bear them up' but rather, taking the three disciples with him, ascends the mountain (which is not described as high). While Moses–Sinai overtones are suggested by Luke's account, they receive nothing like the attention they are given in Matthew. Indeed, mountains do not figure prominently in this Gospel, although Luke is aware that they are associated with revelation and communion with God, particularly in relation to Jesus (6:12; 21:21, 37; 22:39–46).[13] The mountain in this context, as on other occasions in Luke, is a symbol of prayer and Jesus' special relationship with God.[14]

Luke places John's name before James, probably anticipating Acts where the two apostles Peter and John are often linked (e.g Acts 3:1–4:22; 8:14–17; see Luke 22:8);[15] the third apostle, James, is later beheaded by Herod (Acts 12:2). In Luke's Gospel, these three are singled out for a special place within the circle of the twelve, but only in the first half of the Gospel and not to the same extent as in Mark. Their call to discipleship is dramatic, following the miraculous catch of fish (5:1–11);[16] being among the twelve, they are named apostles (6:12–16). The three are the only apostles to witness the raising of Jairus' daughter (8:49–56) and the transfiguration is the last time they are distinguished from the twelve. Unlike Mark, they are not singled out for the apocalyptic discourse (21:5–44) nor for Jesus' agony on the Mount of Olives (22:39–46). As in Matthew, the Lukan disciples are the 'infants' to whom revelation is given (10:21; Matt. 11:25), so privileged and favoured by God that a beatitude is bestowed on them (10:24). Indeed, for Luke, the reason for the limitations in their faith and understanding is that the disciples have not yet received the Spirit. This makes Luke less critical than Mark, yet without denying the disciples misunderstanding.

The Lukan Jesus climbs the mount of transfiguration for the purpose of prayer (*proseuxasthai*). This detail, unique to Luke, makes much more sense of Jesus' ascent up the mountain;[17] he does not go to be transfigured but to pray,[18] drawing the three apostles into the circle of his prayer (see 11:1–13; 22:39–46), a prayer that becomes 'the mother of that blessed vision'.[19] Prayer is a major theme of Luke–Acts. Jesus himself prays frequently in the Gospel, including on one occasion throughout the night,[20] as do the apostles after the ascension.[21] The theme of prayer is closely tied to Luke's emphasis, in both volumes of his work, on the Holy Spirit as the source both of Jesus' power, and later that of the Church. Prayer and the Spirit are interlocking themes at Jesus' baptism which, like the transfiguration, is an epiphany. In Luke's version, Jesus is at prayer when he is baptized and the Holy Spirit descends on him in the form of a dove to 'anoint' him for his ministry (3:21–2).[22] Not only is prayer a major Lukan motif, it also occurs at significant moments or turning points in the narrative, the baptism and transfiguration being two examples. In Acts, the disciples gather in prayer to complete the circle of the twelve and are therefore at prayer – as Luke implies – when the Spirit descends at Pentecost (Acts 1:14; 2:1). Thus, Jesus experiences the transfiguration in the context of intimacy and union with God.[23] Luke underlines the significance of the connection between transfiguration and prayer by repetition: 'and it happened that while he was praying' (9:29). This feature also shows that, in this part of the transfiguration story, Luke's focus is on Jesus himself. What is depicted here is 'the serenity of the Son of Man wrapt in communion with the Father',[24] in preparation for the arduous journey that awaits him.

The wording of Jesus' actual transfiguration is very simple. Avoiding the overt language of metamorphosis, the story speaks of 'the appearance of his face' becoming 'other'.[25] Luke seems to shy away from Hellenistic ideas, and especially pagan tales of humans taking the form of animals or plants (often enough to escape divine persecution).[26] Luke's symbolism parallels the baptism where the same word applies to the Spirit who appears in bodily form as a dove (*eidos*, 3:22). The language reflects Jewish traditions of the faces of the righteous illuminated in the heavenly world, a tradition that extends to the martyrdom of Stephen whose face, before the Sanhedrin, is like that of an angel (Acts 6:15; see Apoc. 1:16; 10:1).[27]

While Luke's description of the change in Jesus' face seems understated, the depiction of his clothing is not. Jesus' garments become blazingly white. The word that Luke uses to describe this change, 'dazzling' (*exastraptôn*), is unusual and dramatic. In this or similar form, Luke uses the word root to describe flashes of lightning or supernatural phenomena:[28] Jesus has a vision of Satan falling like lightning (*astrapên*, 10:18); he speaks of lightning flashing forth in the natural world (*astrapê astraptousa*, 17:24) and a lamp shining forth with its rays (*en astrapê[i]*, 11:36); the two angels are clothed in flashing clothes at the empty tomb (*en esthêti astraptousê[i]*, 24:4), although at the ascension their clothes are described simply as 'white' (*en esthêsesi leukais*, Acts 1:10); on the road to Damascus, a light from heaven flashes around Saul (Paul) as he travels to persecute the Church (*periêstrapsen*, Acts 9:3; *periastrapsai*, Acts 22:6). The language, in its various forms, gives a sense of dramatic radiance that can arise suddenly within nature or from heaven. Here, at the transfiguration, the meaning is clearly the latter. The sense communicated is that of an astonishingly brilliant light flaming forth from Jesus – the radiance of his body shining through his garments in flashes of fire,[29] like light pouring through a window. In general, such imagery is characteristic of apocalyptic traditions, as we have seen, both in relation to God and the righteous whose garments glisten with light at the end time.[30] More generally, the language belongs to the heavenly realm, where white and light are intimately associated with celestial beings, manifestations of divine presence, holiness and beauty.[31] It is ironic that Herod has Jesus arrayed in bright clothing when Jesus appears before him in the passion narrative (*esthêta lampran*, 23:11).[32]

Moses and Elijah are introduced in Luke's story in an unusual way (9:30). Luke uses the exclamation 'behold' to suggest an extraordinary event, beyond human expectation. The reference to 'two men' speaking with Jesus seems at first grammatically awkward, along with the subsequent identification of them as Moses and Elijah (in proper chronological order).[33] This apparent literary clumsiness could indicate that Luke may have depended on another source, possibly older than Mark's (where the 'two men' were originally angels).[34] However, it is more likely that Luke has aligned the transfiguration to the stories of the empty tomb and the ascension, both of which refer to the appearance of 'two men', clearly angels (*andres duo*, Luke 24:4; Acts 1:10). The parallel does not reduce the Lukan transfiguration to an anticipated (or even dislodged) resurrection or ascension story,[35] even though transfiguration, resurrection, ascension and parousia belong together in Luke's theology. In one sense, Luke is indeed already looking to the future in his presentation of Jesus' transfiguration. But Moses and Elijah are also figures of the past, their appearance making visible Israel and its traditions, its election, its hopes and dreams, and its understanding of divine revelation. Both prophets stand for the law,[36] both encounter God dramatically on Mount Horeb/Sinai (Exod. 3; 24; 34; 1 Kgs. 19:11–1), and both meet their ends in mysterious circumstances, Moses being secretly buried (and therefore, for parts of later Judaism, actually translated into heaven,[37] Deut. 34:1–8) and Elijah taken up in a fiery chariot to heaven (2 Kgs. 2:1–12). The effect is to strengthen the impression that the story of Jesus, from beginning to end, is surrounded by heavenly signs and heavenly citizens: Gabriel in the birth stories (1:5–38); the two angels at the end of Luke and beginning of Acts (Luke 24:4–7; Acts 1:10–11); the Holy Spirit throughout both volumes but conspicuous especially at the commencement of each; the voice of God at baptism and transfiguration; and the presence of Moses and Elijah at the transfiguration. For a moment, the reader may indeed wonder whether the two men in Luke's account are angels, but they are quickly identified as these two very human figures of Israel's past, whose lives (and deaths), for Luke, point forward eschatologically to Jesus himself (see 24:27, 44).[38] Moses and Elijah speak together with Jesus (*synelaloun*), conversing on intimate terms, as if they already know him. Jesus' prayer grants him entry into the celestial world.[39]

Luke is explicit in mentioning glory in the transfiguration story, unlike his Synoptic counterparts. Initially, glory occurs in relation to the appearance of Moses and Elijah – 'having appeared in glory' (9:31) – but in the next verse it describes Jesus' appearance which the three disciples witness: 'they saw his glory' (9:32). The language of glory occurs throughout the Gospel – in the verbal form, where people glorify God's mighty acts (e.g. 5:25–6; 7:16; 18:43), and as a noun, where it is an acclamation of praise to God (2:14; 19:38) or indicates the nearness of the heavenly world to earth, associated with light (e.g. 2:9, 32). Glory is offered to, and refused by, Jesus in the temptation narrative (4:6), Luke contrasting 'the proffered devilish glory' with the authentic glory of God.[40] In the scene that precedes the transfiguration, glory depicts the realm of heaven: the Father, the Son of Man and the angels (9:26). Similarly at the transfiguration, the glory signifies the *Shekinah*, the luminous divine dwelling on earth. Light and glory are already closely related concepts in the Old Testament where glory means the powerful and radiant reality of God in its holy otherness and engaging nearness to human life. Especially in the Greek version of the Old Testament, glory (*doxa*) can mean the divine being 'either in its invisible or its perceptible form' – either the essence or manifest presence of God.[41] Mark and Matthew make no direct reference to glory in their accounts of the transfiguration (though it is implied), but in Luke the word symbolizes the celestial abode to which the mountain gives access, and also the divine presence that embraces Jesus. It has both a present and a future dimension.[42] The glory which Moses reflects on Mount Sinai in the Old Testament, which abides on Mount Sion in the temple (Ps. 25:8; Wis. 9:8), and which will be fully manifest in God's future – in the banquet at the end time and the establishing of peace and harmony on the earth (Isa. 11:6–9; 25:6–10a) – is anticipated in the face and raiment of Christ on the mount of transfiguration.[43] The remarkable point here is not that Moses and Elijah are associated with divine glory but that Jesus himself, while still on earth, reflects the brightness of the divine presence, signifying God's visitation to Israel (1:68; 19:44) and prefiguring Christ's future glory. That light and glory have already entered the present, as the canticles in the birth narratives make plain (1:78–9; 2:14, 32).

Luke alone recounts the subject of conversation between the three celestial beings: 'they were speaking of his departure which he was about to fulfil in Jerusalem' (9:31). The word for departure is the unusual *exodos* (meaning literally a 'road out') which usually signifies death, as elsewhere in the biblical world (Wis. 3:2, 6; 2 Pet. 1:15). In the Lukan context, it suggests a wider meaning,[44] confirmed in the use of the strong verb 'fulfil'. The 'exodus' Jesus is to accomplish in Jerusalem is no less than the central events of salvation history. What is to be fulfilled is God's plan for salvation, manifest in the death, resurrection and ascension of Jesus, along with the sending of the Spirit on the gathered Church in Jerusalem, the city of destiny.[45] The word 'exodus' may also have overtones of the departure of the children of Israel from Egypt for the Promised Land,[46] their 'land of destiny'[47] (see Heb. 11:22). If so, the meaning is primarily Christological – it is not the 'exodus' of the disciples that is chiefly under discussion but Jesus' own 'exodus', his path through life and death which is the path of God's visitation.[48] That this will have redemptive, liberating consequences for the disciples is without doubt, but Jesus' experience is Luke's concern at this point. Just as in the temptation narrative Jesus lives out Israel's history, so he takes up into himself Israel's journey, creating a new route by which 'all flesh' will be saved (3:6). This motif is

similar to Matthew's theme of Jesus replaying Israel's story and rendering obedience in place of disobedience. Thus by his 'exodus' the Lukan
Jesus 'leads the way for his people out of the world and into heaven'.[49]
Partly at least, the transfiguration functions as a confirmation of Jesus'
destiny as he prepares to turn and face Jerusalem.[50]

In the next section, the attention shifts from Jesus' experience to that
of the disciples (9:32–6). Luke expands Mark's narrative at this point, so
that Peter's suggestion of making three tents is delayed. Instead, the three
disciples are described as 'heavy with sleep' (*bebarêmenoi hypnô[i]*, 9:32).
It is unclear whether this means that they have actually fallen asleep and
so missed the conversation between Jesus, Moses and Elijah – waking up
to perceive the 'glory' and the presence of the two men – or whether they
are sleepy and later roused to full wakefulness. The difference is not great
in any case. One thing the description does suggest is that the transfiguration, in Luke's mind, occurs at night, as Jesus' prayer often does (6:12).[51]
More significantly, the drowsiness of the disciples prefigures the Mount of
Olives where, immediately before his arrest, Jesus prays for the strength
to comply with the will of God while the disciples sleep (22:39–46). There
too the disciples are in the presence of 'the mysterious and incomprehensible'.[52] In Mark's account, the Gethsemane story has the same inner
group of three disciples who attempt to remain awake but fail to realize
the spiritual danger which lies before them (Mark 14:32–42). In the Lukan
equivalent, Jesus' first instruction to the disciples is to pray that they may
be spared the 'time of trial' (22:40; see 11:4), while he departs some
distance and prays for the cup to be taken from him, though only in accord
with the Father's will (22:41–2).[53] Luke describes the disciples' sleep sympathetically as arising from 'grief' (*lupê*, 22:45) and Jesus reiterates the
command to pray with which the scene began (22:46). In this way, the two
mountain scenes – the glory and the agony – overlap in significant ways.
Just as the first sets Jesus' death at the centre of the manifestation of
glory, so the second shows Jesus' fidelity in prayer, reminding the reader
of the glory of the transfiguration in the context of agony, an agony
that will lead assuredly to the joy of the resurrection (24:52). The motif of
sleep at the transfiguration is thus Luke's way of tying together the two
scenes and explaining the disciples' confusion and misunderstanding. At
the transfiguration, however, they do not miss out entirely on the sight
of the glory. What they see fulfils the promise of 'those standing here',
the glory of God (9:27).[54] Now it is clear that the glory of the three
heavenly figures belongs primarily to Jesus; the two greatest prophets

of Israel's past are relegated to second place.

Peter's words show misunderstanding yet also indicate his awareness of the lustrous beauty and goodness of the transfiguration: 'it is good for us to be here' (*kalon*, 9:33). His suggestion that three tents be erected to house the celestial beings is worded differently from Mark. Peter's use of 'Rabbi' becomes 'Master', a more exalted mode of address that is characteristic of Luke.[55] Peter addresses Jesus with the same title on two other occasions in the Gospel (5:5; 8:45); the disciples as a group use it in the boat (8:24); the apostle John employs it soon after the transfiguration (9:49); and the blind man at the end of the journey calls upon Jesus in the same terms (17:13). 'Master', in other words, is a mode of address used by the Lukan disciples to signify Jesus' divinely-given power and authority. Luke again indicates his sympathy for Peter, even in his lack of understanding; the transfiguration is beyond the capacity of the disciples (at this stage) to grasp. Peter's suggestion, therefore, is not to be taken seriously. Though it displays the limitations of his awareness, his words demonstrate also his sense of the splendour of the transfiguration.

It is significant that Peter's suggestion occurs just as Moses and Elijah are departing ('while they were departing'). More clearly than the other evangelists, Luke provides a reason for Peter's proposal: he does not want the two men to depart. The question still remains as to why Peter thinks these shelters will enable him 'to freeze the moment'.[56] The candidates for the Old Testament background are the same as for Mark and Matthew, as is also the conclusion: Peter's suggestion is not at all clear, even with all the background possibilities before us. There are three traditions within Judaism that might explain Peter's suggestion. One is the feast of Tabernacles, originally a harvest festival with later eschatological overtones, during the celebration of which the people inhabited tents or huts made of leaves and branches (Lev. 23:33–6; Deut. 16:13–15).[57] This seems the least likely explanation, as Peter would hardly think to omit himself and his fellow disciples from such a celebration, and should propose the erecting of six tents rather than three. The second is the tent of meeting where God spoke to Moses in the wilderness (Exod. 33:7–11; Deut. 31:14–15), the problem being why Peter would suggest three tents rather than one. Even if he is erroneously placing the three celestial figures on the same level, the tent in the wilderness was primarily for God's (temporary) residence and certainly not for Moses himself. The third is the most explicitly eschatological, namely, that Peter is recalling the tradition of the dwellings of the righteous in the heavenly world at the end time, a theory that coheres with the apocalyptic dimensions of the change in Jesus' face and raiment.[58] It is possible that Luke's earlier reference to Moses and Elijah appearing 'in glory' means that their raiment is similar to Jesus', which would suit this theory. However, upon waking, the disciples see a glory that belongs to Jesus alone and not to his companions. Whatever the physical appearance of Moses and Elijah (and Luke is rather vague), they are by no means on the same level as Jesus himself. The most likely explanation, as for the other Gospels, is that Peter himself is unsure of his own meaning and simply wants to prolong the experience by providing whatever is to hand to compel them to stay. Luke's description of Peter as 'not knowing what he was saying' accords with this view, suggesting that the reader cannot, and does not need to, know what Peter intends by his proposal.[59]

In addition to Jesus' transfiguration and the appearance of Moses and Elijah are two further heavenly signs, the cloud and the voice (9:34–5). Both symbols signify the intervention of God, their function being to explain and clarify the earlier signs and show their impact on the disciples.[60] In Luke's account (as in Matthew) it is clear that the cloud interrupts Peter's proposal, effectively muffling him and preventing him from speaking further (Matt. 17:5), while stressing also the inappropriateness of his request. Ironically, the cloud itself 'makes a tent' to overshadow those present;[61] Peter's suggestion is unnecessary since 'God's own dwelling comes to earth and accommodates his people'.[62] As in the other two Gospels, the cloud signifies the mysterious presence of God, revealed and concealed at the same time, both dimensions equally overwhelming: 'the awesome and fearful presence of God is both hidden and revealed by the presence of the cloud.'[63] In the Old Testament, the cloud is already associated with divine glory, especially in relation to the tabernacle/temple.[64]

It is not entirely clear in Luke who actually enters the cloud. The disciples, Luke says, are afraid as '*they* entered into the cloud' (9:34), but nothing indicates who 'they' are. In favour of the view that the disciples are excluded is the fact that the divine voice speaks 'out of' (*ek*) the cloud, suggesting that the disciples are outside. On the other hand, it is hard to see why the disciples would be frightened unless they too were entering the cloud. The sentence is more awkward if the two personal pronouns (the one implied in the verb, the other expressed) refer to two different groups: 'they [the disciples] were afraid as they [Jesus, Moses and Elijah] entered the cloud.' On balance, it is more likely that all six enter the cloud.[65] The disciples' fear would then be an example, not of separation anxiety, but of 'holy fear' at the presence of God, like the shepherds at the angelic announcement of Jesus' birth (2:9). If the disciples do enter the cloud, as seems likely, Luke is depicting the presence of God as something that is both beyond the disciples' comprehension and at the same time embracing of them, with all their limitations. They are enfolded in the divine embrace, even while it silences them and reduces them to fear and awe.

There is a further dimension to the cloud that is implicit in Luke's account. In the annunciation to Mary, the same verb, 'overshadow', is used in relation to her miraculous pregnancy (*episkiazein*).[66] The angel assures her that

the Holy Spirit will come upon you
and the power from on high will overshadow you;
therefore that which is born will be holy and called Son of God. (1:35)

In the first two lines, we have an example of synonymous Hebrew parallelism where the two statements are saying much the same thing, though in slightly different wording. Here the overshadowing is associated with the Spirit who descends on Mary, filling her, body and soul, with the presence of God. Gabriel, who 'stands before God' (1:19), represents the voice of God, confirming Mary as the recipient of divine favour (1:28) and her child as the Son of God (1:32), chosen to exercise God's everlasting dominion. If it is right to see a parallel between this scene and the transfiguration, the cloud by association is linked to the enveloping presence of the Holy Spirit. Drawing the baptism into this circle, we see that there too the Spirit descends in tangible form to anoint Jesus – this time, as a dove – and the divine voice speaks, in similar wording to the transfiguration, confirming Jesus as the Son of God (3:21–2). In each case, there is a descending or overshadowing presence from heaven, associated explicitly in two of the three cases with the Spirit of God. The same is suggested by the transfiguration, with its symbolism of the overarching cloud and the solemn, divine utterance that issues from it. To the attentive reader, the cloud signifies the descent and overshadowing of the Spirit.

The voice that issues from the cloud, unlike that of the baptism, addresses the three apostles directly, confirming Jesus' identity as it shines forth in his face and clothing (9:35). The wording is similar but not identical to Mark. The one difference is that, in place of 'beloved', Luke prefers to use 'chosen' (*eklelegêmenos*, 9:35).[67] The two notions are by no means dissimilar. The passage from Isaiah from which Luke's designation comes incorporates both epithets: the servant is beloved of and chosen by God (*eklektos*), anointed by God's Spirit (Isa. 42:1–2; see Luke 4:18). As the true Servant, Jesus must not only obey but also suffer in order to establish God's righteousness and bring blessing to Israel.[68] On the cross, Jesus is mocked precisely as God's Chosen One (*eklektos*, 23:35), a taunt that is ironically true. God's election of Jesus is closely linked with the election of Israel; indeed, Jesus symbolizes Israel as God's chosen people and fulfils the prophecies concerning Israel's ancient saving rôle which, in Luke's eyes, extends to 'all flesh', through the gift of the Spirit (cf. Acts 2:17). By means of his death and resurrection, the Servant who has suffered is exalted forever at God's right hand, as both Messiah and Lord (Acts 2:32–6).

As we have seen, the divine voice declares Jesus to be God's Son, paralleling the annunciation to Mary and Jesus' baptism. The title is infrequent in Luke, unlike Matthew, with 'Messiah' and 'Lord' being more numerous throughout Luke–Acts. Yet it is still an important part of Luke's Christology, with royal if not divine overtones (Ps. 2:7; cf. Acts 13:33): 'an unparalleled approach to God and his rule is implicated in Jesus' identity as Son.'[69] Within the Galilean part of Jesus' ministry there is a circular arrangement of declarations of Jesus' identity: at the beginning and end, he is pronounced Messiah and Son of God – by God (Son of God, 3:22), by Jesus himself (Messiah, 4:18), by Peter (Messiah, 9:20) and by God (Son of God, 9:35).[70] Jesus is God's Son by virtue of his virginal conception (1:31–5), his genealogy which goes back, via his adoption by Joseph, to Adam – confirming his oneness with humanity (3:23–38) – and his temptations, where his filial dependence on God is tested and vindicated (4:1–13). The strangely Johannine saying about the Father and the Son is present in Luke, as in Matthew (10:22; see Matt. 11:27), though on the early part of Jesus' journey: 'All things have been handed over to me by my Father, and no-one knows who the Son is except the Father, nor who the Father is except the Son and the one to whom the Son wishes to reveal him' (10:22). This demonstrates Jesus' unique connection to God in relation to revelation: 'It is through Jesus and only through Jesus, that people come to know the Father as he is.'[71] Similarly, in Acts, Paul proclaims Jesus as Son of God in his first preaching following his conversion (Acts 9:20; 13:33). Here at the transfiguration the title conveys a sense of 'Jesus' special divine filiation' and exclusive role in divine revelation.[72] Within the embrace of the cloud, the divine voice confirms Jesus' identity as Son and Servant at the point where his journey to Jerusalem is about to commence, just as his identity was confirmed in his baptism as his ministry was about to begin.

The three disciples are commanded to listen to Jesus as God's Chosen Son, an injunction that brings us back to the beginning with the mention of Jesus' words ('after these words', 9:28). Luke changes the word order here, making the reference to Jesus emphatic: 'to him, listen'. This harkening to Jesus – which means listening and obeying – is especially pertinent immediately before the journey to Jerusalem in the light of Jesus' teaching. Already Mary has been portrayed as the exemplar of this kind of obedient, faithful listening (1:38, 45; see 11:27–8; 24:8).[73] Luke's concern is primarily with the saving events in Jerusalem in the light of Jesus' teaching and their implications for discipleship and the life of the Church. Significantly, Luke's wording immediately before the second passion prediction reinforces the same message: 'Put into your ears these words ...' (9:44).[74] The context indicates that the disciples cannot bear to receive the message of Jesus' suffering and betrayal, because, says Luke sympathetically, it was hidden from them and they were too afraid to ask (9:45). The divine voice portrays Jesus in the pattern of the prophet-like-Moses whose words are those of God (Deut. 18:18). At the same time, Jesus is greater than Moses or any other prophet,[75] as the transfiguration makes plain, his identity gathering up yet transcending all the Old Testament designations that Luke employs. Like John the Baptist, Moses and Elijah belong to the old order whose task is to symbolize the new, even as the old passes away.[76] Jesus' voice, above all others, articulates the voice of God throughout Luke–Acts, in his ministry, his journey to Jerusalem, his resurrection appearances and his ascension to God's right hand. Thus Jesus, and Jesus alone, is 'heaven's Son and Chosen One to whom human beings must now listen for their relation to God's kingdom'.[77]

The voice of God, which proclaims Jesus and which is embodied in him, has the last word in Luke's story (9:36). The signs of the transfiguration – the dazzling clothes, the presence of Moses and Elijah and their discourse with Jesus, the cloud and the voice – all vanish and Jesus is left alone with his disciples. The glory is not yet permanent until Jesus' 'exodus': until the salvation events of his departure, foretold in the Old Testament and achieved via the long journey to Jerusalem. For Luke, glory is linked to the beginning – the divine visitation – and also to the end – the 'exodus' – but the transfiguration stands in the middle as a vantage point that looks

backwards and forwards: to the birth stories and beyond in the Old
Testament Scriptures, and to the empty tomb and the ascension, where,
as Stephen sees in his martyrdom, Jesus stands in glory at God's right
hand (Acts 7:55–6). In Luke, the glory is not simply a future event, but is
associated with the past and already begins to permeate the present. The
transfiguration permits the reader a glimpse from the mountain peak into
the divine glory which is the goal of both visitation and journey. Jesus'
faithful obedience, his dependence on God and his readiness to suffer in
surrendering his whole self to God, re-enact the story of Israel, extending
that saving narrative to the ends of the earth. Luke's Gospel is embraced
by glory at the beginning, middle and end. In between is the hard road to
Jerusalem that Jesus willingly takes and that leaves him, at the conclusion
of the transfiguration, ready to go where the Father directs him.

Luke's account of the crucifixion, so markedly different from the other
Gospels, captures this willing obedience and presents the cross as central
to God's eschatological plan of salvation.[78] Jesus' last words, in the context
of the apocalyptic signs of the three-hour darkness and the tearing of the
veil – portraying the 'ominous effect' of Jesus' death[79] – are not a cry of
dereliction but a confident, even passionate, surrender of his life to the
Father (23:46; see Mark 15:34). There is no sense here of a divine absence.
Jesus' earlier promise to the penitent thief (23:42–3), along with his
prayer for his executioners (23:34),[80] portray him as the one through
whom salvation comes. The real epiphany, for Luke, lies not so much in
the faith-declaration of the centurion, which confirms Jesus as both innocent and righteous (*dikaios*, 23:47),[81] but rather in the events associated
with the resurrection. The epiphany at the empty tomb, where once more
we find frightened disciples, is inconclusive, leaving the women believing
and the eleven in disbelief, despite the message of the 'two men in dazzling
raiment' (24:4–7, 11). At Emmaus, the two disciples recognize Jesus in the
glory of broken hearts and burning bread (24:31–2); in Jerusalem, the
disciples' fear is comforted by his gift of peace (24:36). The epiphany con-
tinues until Bethany and the moment of his ascension – spanning the two
volumes of Luke–Acts – where the risen Christ ascends to heaven, spread-
ing his hands in blessing (24:50–1), after promising the gift of the Spirit.
Here too the epiphany of his presence and authority becomes an apocalyptic vision of the future, to be realized to a considerable extent in the life
of the Church. In his ascension on the cloud, Jesus indicates the manner
and verity of his return, as the two men in white robes proclaim (Acts
1:9–11). The glory of Christ at the transfiguration prepares the disciples

(and the reader) for the glory of Easter, ascension, Pentecost and parousia.

At this point, therefore, it is the transfigured face of Jesus – the face that soon will be set towards Jerusalem (9:51)[82] – as much as the terror of the cloud and the divine voice, that overcomes the three disciples on the mountain. It would be a mistake to interpret the voice as the climax of the narrative. Its function is to interpret the visible phenomena associated with the transfiguration and set them within an explicitly Christological framework.[83] The view that the real heart of the transfiguration is the divine voice downgrades the importance of 'seeing' in the experience of the disciples and makes peripheral the central symbols of the narrative. The disciples do not respond just to the speaking but to the glory and beauty of Jesus' metamorphosis. Both the seeing and the hearing are equally over-whelming for them: they 'reported to no-one in those days *anything of what they had seen*' (9:36).[84] Note here the priority of what they *see*, expli-cated by what they *hear* from within the cloud. The change in Jesus, the sight of Moses and Elijah, the entry into the divine cloud, are as impossi-ble for them to grasp as the subject of conversation or the direct interven-tion of God. Whereas in Mark and Matthew the disciples' silence is the result of Jesus' instructions (Mark 9:9; Matt. 17:9), in Luke it is the disci-ples' spontaneous response to an event that, at this stage ('in those days'), is quite literally ineffable.[85] The silence of the three Lukan apostles, like that of the three women disciples at the empty tomb in Mark's Gospel (Mark 16:8), is understood as temporary – in Luke's case, explicitly so: 'Only by truly listening to Jesus will they be able to break their silence and report in the days to come what they experienced in the transfiguration epiphany.'[86]

Jesus does not instruct the Lukan disciples to keep silent because there is no need: they have no desire and no capacity as yet to speak. Speech can only come after the events in Jerusalem, culminating in the gift of the Spirit, which Jesus will send upon them (3:16; 24:49), when their speech will become miraculous (Acts 2:4). In the meantime, unlike Jesus himself, the three disciples have missed the reassurance implied in the transfigura-tion which functions as 'a foreshadowing of the ultimate victory'[87] and which discloses the glory that will eventuate in and through Jesus' depar-ture.[88] Their descent down the mountain on the next day leads them into a situation of desperate need (9:37–43): the demon-possession of an only son whom the other disciples have failed to heal. Jesus' exorcism of this child leads the crowd to extol the greatness of God (9:43; see 1:46), a great-ness already visible, in spectacular ways, at the transfiguration. By this connection between the two stories, Luke intimates that the glory of God is profoundly healing and restoring of human life.

Luke's story of the transfiguration is a powerful one in its own right – significantly different from Mark in a number of pertinent details, even while retaining many of the same symbols. Like Mark, the narrative functions as an epiphany of Jesus' identity as the Chosen Son, revealed in beauty and power on the mountain, and as an apocalyptic vision of God's joyful future, fulfilled in him. The addition of Jesus' prayer as the theological context of the transfiguration, and the relating of the subject of conversation between Jesus, Moses and Elijah, give a stronger focus to the experience of Jesus himself, preparing and strengthening him for what lies ahead. Luke emphasizes the unity that Jesus has with God, displayed in his life of prayer. As Son and Servant of the Father, whose will he obeys in total commitment and trust, Jesus is confirmed in his identity and in the path of redemptive suffering he must tread, entering radically into 'the limitations of this age' in order to attain eschatological glory in the joy and triumph of the resurrection.[89]

The disciples are equally important for Luke's story. The transfiguration implies the journey they too are required to take, a journey in company with Jesus that will lead to 'the reshaping of Israel as God's people'.[90] Their experience begins with their somnolence before the glory that meets their eyes, a feature that links the transfiguration to the story of Jesus' agony on the Mount of Olives, where the disciples also sleep while Jesus prays. Their reactions are inadequate in Luke's transfiguration but understandably so, given the dazzling nature of Jesus' glory on the mountain and the enormity of what he is about to do in turning resolutely towards Jerusalem. The cloud and the voice signify the mystery yet immanence of God, symbolized elsewhere in Luke by the Spirit who reveals Jesus' identity and inspires the proclaiming of the gospel. The silence at the end of the story is the result of the disciples' own volition, but it dramatizes the ineffability of the event and the impossibility of the apostles' speech until the day when 'power from on high' descends upon them (24:48), empowers them for mission to 'the ends of the earth'. Here on the mountain the three disciples are truly blessed in what their eyes have seen and their ears heard. What they perceive in the transfigured body of Jesus and in the depths of the cloud is something for which 'many prophets and kings' profoundly longed (10:23–4) – the enlightenment, through Israel, of the Gentiles.

Notes

1 Schweizer, E., *The Good News According to Luke* (trans. D. E. Green), SPCK, London, 1984, 159.

2 Heil, J. P., *The Transfiguration of Jesus: Narrative Meaning and Function of Mark 9:2–8, Matt 17:1–8 and Luke 9:28–36*, Editrice Pontificio Istituto Biblico, Rome, 2000, 51–73, Tannehill, R. C., *Luke*, Abingdon, Nashville, TN, 1996, 160, Tiede, L., *Luke*, Augsburg, Minneapolis, MN, 1988, 188, and Craddock, F. B., *Luke*, John Knox, Louisville, KY, 1990, 132–3.

3 Neirynck, F., 'Minor Agreements Matthew–Luke in the Transfiguration Story', in Hoffmann, P. (ed.), *Orientierung an Jesus: Zur Theologie der Synoptiker*, Herder, Freiburg, 1973, 253–66.

4 For this view, see Reid, B., *The Transfiguration: A Source- and Redaction-Critical Study of Luke 9:28–36 (Cahiers de la Revue Biblique)*, J. Gabalda, Paris, 1993, 31–94, and Murphy-O'Connor, J., 'What Really Happened at the Transfiguration?' *Bible Review 3*, 1987.

5 Most commentators reject a second source; e.g. Fitzmyer, J. A., *The Gospel According to Luke*, 2 vols, Doubleday, Garden City, NY, 1981, 1985, vol. 1, 791–2, and Marshall, I. H., *The Gospel of Luke*, Eerdmans, Grand Rapids, MI, 1978, 380–1.

6 Luke omits Mark 6:45–8:26 to keep Herod's questioning together with the more pointed questions of Jesus; see Talbert, C. H., *Reading Luke: A Literary and Theological Commentary on the Third Gospel*, Crossroad, New York, 1982, 102, and Ringe, S. H., 'Luke 9:28–36: The Beginning of an Exodus', *Semeia* 28, 1983, 93.

7 Fitzmyer, *Luke*, vol. 1, 793.

8 The journey is longer than in Mark (Luke 9:51–19:27; cf. Mark 8:22–10:52), including sayings that Luke shares with Matthew (Q) and his own material.

9 Marshall, *op. cit.*, 385. See Luke 9:51, 56, 57–62; 10:1, 38; 13:22; 14:25; 17:11; 18:31, 35, 43; 19:1, 11, 28–9, 37, 41.

10 Nolland, J., *Luke 9:21–18:34* (vol. 2), Word Books, Dallas, TX, 1993, 496, 500, 504; Tannehill, *op. cit.*, 162.

11 Luke gives no particular location to this conversation (see Mark 8:27; Matt. 16:13).

12 Marshall, *op. cit.*, 382. Symbolic suggestions have been proposed, such as the 'eighth day' of creation (Perry, J. M., *Exploring the Transfigura-*

tion Story, Sheed & Ward, Kansas City, MO, 1993, 50–1), but these have little support in the Lukan writings.

13 Luke, if we follow the correct text, does not refer to the mountain in the temptation (4:5), and instead of the Sermon on the Mount there is the (much shorter) Sermon on the Plain (Luke 6:17–49); the people of Nazareth try to throw Jesus off a mountain after his first sermon (4:29).

14 Fitzmyer, *Luke*, vol. 1, 798.

15 Luke follows the traditional order at 6:14, but in Acts 1:13 again has 'John and James'.

16 Note, however, that Andrew is not mentioned in this episode and only the three leave their boats and follow Jesus (5:10–11; cf. Mark 1:16–20).

17 Nolland, *Luke* 9:21–18:34, 496–7, sees Luke's reference to prayer as more logical than Mark.

18 Reid, *op. cit.*, 103–4.

19 Gregory Palamas, *Homily* 34, in McGuckin, J. A., *The Transfiguration of Christ in Scripture and Tradition*, Edwin Mellen, Lewiston, NY, 1986, 230.

20 Luke 3:21; 5:16; 6:12; 9:18; 10:21; 11:1–4; 22:32, 41–2; 23:46. As Harrington, W. J., *Luke, Gracious Theologian: The Jesus of Luke*, Columba Press, Dublin, 1997, 89, notes, Jesus' prayer (Ps. 31:5) shows that 'the surrender of his life to the Father was a prayer' (see Acts 7:59). Jesus' prayer from the cross has textual problems (23:34); see Metzger, B. M., *A Textual Commentary on the Greek New Testament*, 2nd edn, United Bible Societies, London, 1975, 180.

21 See Luke 24:53; Acts 1:14, 24; 4:24–31; 6:4, 6; 12:5, 12; 13:3.

22 The baptism of Jesus by John the Baptist in Luke is secondary to his anointing by the Spirit (3:21).

23 Further on this theme, see Crump, D., *Jesus the Intercessor: Prayer and Christology in Luke–Acts*, J. C. B. Mohr (Paul Siebeck), Tübingen, 1992, 42–8.

24 Ramsay, M., *The Glory of God and the Transfiguration of Christ*, 2nd edn, Darton, Longman & Todd, London, 1967, 121.

25 This is not a 'divine passive', unlike the verb 'was transfigured' (Mark 9:2/Matt. 17:2). Yet here too Jesus 'is not acting but being acted on' (Craddock, *op. cit.*, 135).

26 McGuckin, *op. cit.*, 57–65, Plummer, A. et al. (eds), *A Critical and Exegetical Commentary on the Gospel According to St. Luke*, 5th edn,

T. & T. Clark, Edinburgh, 1922, 251, and Marshall, *op. cit.*, 483. The Romans produced two great works on transfiguration: Ovid, *Metamorphoses* (c. 8 AD) and Apuleius, *Metamorphoses (The Golden Ass,* c. 170 AD*)*. The New Testament's view of metamorphosis, however, is very different; see Liefeld, W. L., 'Transfigure, Transfiguration, Transform', in Brown, C. (ed.), *The New International Dictionary of New Testament Theology,* vol. 3, 861–3.

27 For stories from the desert of the faces of early saints illuminated by light or fire, see Nes, S., *The Uncreated Light: An Iconographical Study of the Transfiguration in the Eastern Church,* Eastern Christian Publications, Fairfax, VA, 2002, 65–6, 95–6.

28 Fitzmyer, *Luke,* vol. 1, 799, and Foerster, W., '*Astrapê*', in Kittel, G. (ed.), *Theological Dictionary of the New Testament,* vol. 1, Eerdmans, Grand Rapids, MI, 1964, 505.

29 Marshall, *op. cit.*, 383.

30 E.g. Dan. 10:6; 4 Ezra 2:39; 1 Enoch 62:15–16; 104:2; 2 Enoch 22:8–10; 2 Baruch 51:3–10.

31 See Dan. 7:9; 2 Macc. 11:8; Apoc. 7:9, 13–14; 19:14; 1 Enoch 14:20; 71:1.

32 Heil, *op. cit.*, 302–3.

33 Plummer, et al. *St Luke,* 251, suggest that 'who' in verse 30 means 'who were none others than'.

34 Reid, *op. cit.*, 39–40.

35 Fitzmyer, *Luke,* vol. 1, 795–6.

36 In Luke 24, Moses stands for both prophets and law (24:27, 44). For the traditional view, see Plummer, *St Luke,* 251, and Craddock, *op. cit.*, 134.

37 See, e.g. Philo, *Questions on Genesis* 1.8.

38 Nolland, *Luke 9:21–18:34,* 498–9, sees Moses as the 'predecessor' and Elijah the 'precursor' of Jesus, one pointing to the past and the other the future (cf. Mal. 4:4–5). Luke associates Elijah with Jesus (4:25–6; 9:19) and John the Baptist (1:17; 9:7–9).

39 Talbert, *op. cit.*, 103–4.

40 Trites, A. A., 'The Transfiguration in the Theology of Luke: Some Redactional Links', in Hurst, L. D. and Wright, N. T. (eds), *The Glory of Christ in the New Testament,* Clarendon, Oxford, 1987, 76.

41 Kittel, G. and von Rad, G., '*Doxa*', in Kittel, G. (ed.), *Theological Dictionary of the New Testament,* vol. 2, Eerdmans, Grand Rapids, MI, 1964, 245.

42 Reid, *op. cit.*, 115.

43 Nolland, *Luke 9:21–18:34*, 418.

44 Luke uses the opposite word, *eisodos*, to refer to the beginning of Jesus' ministry (Acts 13:24).

45 Reid, *op. cit.*, 126, Marshall, *op. cit.*, 384–5, Nolland, *Luke 9:21–18:34*, 503, and Tannehill, *op. cit.*, 161; against this, see Michaelis, W., '*Eisodos, Exodos, Diexodos*', in Kittel, G. (ed.), *Theological Dictionary of the New Testament*, vol. 5, Eerdmans, Grand Rapids, MI, 1967a, 107.

46 Caird, G. B., *Saint Luke*, Penguin Books, Harmondsworth, 1963, 132, and Byrne, B., *The Hospitality of God: A Reading of Luke's Gospel*, Liturgical Press, Collegeville, MN, 2000, 89–90; especially Ringe, S. H., *Luke*, Westminster/John Knox, Louisville, KY, 1995, 141, and Ringe, 'Luke 9:28–36', 83–99.

47 Fitzmyer, *Luke*, vol. 1, 794.

48 Nolland, *Luke 9:21–18:34*, 499–500.

49 Marshall, *op. cit.*, 380.

50 Nolland, *Luke 9:21–18:34*, 503.

51 Marshall, *op. cit.*, 383. John Chrysostom sees the disciples' sleep as caused by the radiance of the light which darkens their eyes: *Homily 56 on Matthew 17*, 3, in McGuckin, *op. cit.*, 175.

52 Schweizer, *op. cit.*, 160.

53 See especially Kenny, A., 'The Transfiguration and the Agony in the Garden', *Catholic Biblical Quarterly* 19, 1957, 448–52, who also points to the parallels with the Lord's Prayer.

54 Fitzmyer, *Luke*, vol. 1, 791–2.

55 Reid, *op. cit.*, 133.

56 Nolland, *Luke 9:21–18:34*, 501.

57 Fitzmyer, *Luke*, vol. 1, 801, and Tannehill, *op. cit.*, 162.

58 See 1 Enoch 39:3–8 and Testament of Abraham A 20:13–14; so Marshall, *op. cit.*, 386–7.

59 Heil, *op. cit.*, 118–20.

60 This view avoids the problem of seeing them in competition (see Nolland, *Luke 9:21–18:34*, 492–3).

61 Heil, *op. cit.*, 138.

62 Marshall, *op. cit.*; see Schweizer, *op. cit.*, 161.

63 Nolland, *Luke 9:21–18:34*, 504.

64 See Exod. 16:10; 24:15–18; 40:34; 1 Kgs. 8:10–11; Ezek. 10:4; 2 Macc. 2:8. There is no indication that Moses and Elijah travel on the cloud (see Reid, *op. cit.*, 137).

65 *Ibid.*, 137, Nolland, *Luke 9:21–18:34*, 501, and Tiede, *op. cit.*, 190;

against this, see Heil, *op. cit.*, 130–1, 266–71. In Acts 5:15 Peter literally heals by *overshadowing* the sick, a power associated with the Spirit.

66 See Ambrose, *Exposition on Luke*, c.7.18, in McGuckin, *op. cit.*, 268.

67 This seems to be the original wording of the text; see Metzger, *op. cit.*, 148.

68 Marshall, *op. cit.*, 388, and Tiede, *op. cit.*, 190–1. See Isa. 42:1–4; 44:1–5; 45:4; 52:13–53:12.

69 Nolland, J., *Luke 1–9:20* (vol. 1), Word Books, Dallas, TX, 1989, 164.

70 Kingsbury, J. D., *Conflict in Luke: Jesus, Authorities, Disciples*, Fortress, Minneapolis, MN, 1991, 54.

71 Morris, L., *Luke*, 2nd edn, Inter-Varsity Press, Leicester, 1988, 204. On the problems of this verse, see Marshall, *op. cit.*, 435–8.

72 Reid, *op. cit.*, 140.

73 Heil, *op. cit.*, 288.

74 Kingsbury, *op. cit.*, 55.

75 Luke sees Jesus' ministry as prophetic (Fitzmyer, *Luke*, vol. 1, 213–15); yet it transcends that of the prophet. Caird, *op. cit.*, 133, says that, unlike others prophets, Jesus treads an untrodden path; see Kingsbury, *op. cit.*, 53. For the view that Jesus is primarily a prophet, see Tuckett, C. M., *Luke*, Sheffield Academic Press, Sheffield, 1996, 81–5.

76 Caird, *op. cit.*, 133.

77 Fitzmyer, *Luke*, vol. 1, 794.

78 See Doble, P., *The Paradox of Salvation: Luke's Theology of the Cross*, Cambridge University Press, Cambridge, 1996, 235–7.

79 Fitzmyer, *Luke*, vol. 2, 1514.

80 If this verse is part of the Lukan text, which is debatable.

81 On the Christology of this declaration, see Doble, *op. cit.*, 226–32.

82 Heil, *op. cit.*, 286.

83 Reid, *op. cit.*, 98, sees the form of the transfiguration as a 'correction pronouncement story'.

84 The perfect tense of the verb 'to see' (*heôrakan*) suggests continuity of seeing; Marshall, *op. cit.*, 389. Luke stresses sight in the transfiguration story (Crump, *op. cit.*, 45–7).

85 Schweizer, *op. cit.*, 161.

86 Heil, *op. cit.*, 279.

87 Trites, *op. cit.*, 80.

88 Byrne, *op. cit.*, 90.

89 Talbert, *op. cit.*, 105.

90 Fitzmyer, *Luke*, vol. 1, 795.

4

The Transfiguration in 2 Peter

16 For not by following cleverly contrived myths did we make known to you the power and coming [*parousia*] of our Lord Jesus Christ, but after becoming eyewitnesses of his greatness. 17 For having received from God the Father honour and glory, a voice of this kind was conveyed to him by the majestic Glory: 'My Son, my Beloved, this is in whom I have taken delight.' 18 And this voice we ourselves heard conveyed from heaven while being with him on the holy mountain.

(2 Peter 1:16–18)

It is perhaps surprising that the story of the transfiguration – so characteristic of the Synoptic Gospels – should suddenly appear in the middle of one of the lesser known New Testament letters. Yet the second epistle of Peter narrates the same story, though in much abbreviated form and in the context of discourse rather than narrative. While couched in unfamiliar language and imagery, the abridged form of the transfiguration according to 2 Peter incorporates the mountain setting, the metamorphosis of Jesus, the voice declaring Jesus to be the Son and the apostolic witnesses. The theological accent of the symbolism is firmly, indeed almost exclusively, on the anticipation of God's future in Christ. Moreover, instead of the resurrection functioning as the promise of eschatological glory, as elsewhere in the New Testament, the author of 2 Peter prefers to use the transfiguration to the same effect – so much so that the transfiguration in this account lies at the core of the apostolic deposit of faith.

In more general terms, 2 Peter purports to be a letter written by the apostle Peter to an unspecified group of believers (1:1; see 3:1). The letter is more like a testament than anything else, a kind of farewell speech summing up the hopes and perspective of Peter as he prepares to depart the world (1:13–15).[1] The focus, as with all such testaments in the biblical world, is on the dangers and challenges faced by the community that will remain after his departure. Given the educated style of the Greek – very different from what we would expect of a Galilean fisherman – the letter is probably pseudonymous, that is, written in the name of Peter some time after his demise, this being a recognized form of literature in the ancient world.[2] There is a distinct possibility, however, that traditions stemming from Peter himself have been used (perhaps by someone who knew Peter and worked with him),[3] prominent among these being the transfiguration story. This means that – to use the categories of modern literary criticism – the 'implied author', the author within the text itself, is the apostle Peter, while the actual flesh-and-blood author, standing outside the text, is someone else, though not necessarily unconnected with the historical figure and teaching of Peter.[4] The epistle was probably composed towards the end of the first century, perhaps in Rome.

The implied author begins the epistle (or testament) by encouraging his readers to remain faithful to their calling (1:3–11), in order to attain the kingdom, and by reminding them of the apostolic testimony on which their faith is based (1:12–15). He quotes the transfiguration story as the grounds for the apostolic witness, and directs his readers' attention to the prophetic message. By this he refers primarily to the Old Testament writings, but also extends it to the apostolic teachings (1:19–21). From there he goes on to expose the 'false prophets' and 'false teachers' (2:1) whose teaching, in the eyes of 2 Peter, is dangerous and destructive, propagated by people who have wandered far from the knowledge of Jesus Christ and who lead others astray (2:1–22). In the end it becomes clear that the real theological contention between 2 Peter and his opponents is that of the parousia, the future coming of the Lord, which certain teachers and prophets within the Christian community deny (3:1–13). The readers of the epistle, however, are challenged to believe and live out of the hope of the parousia (3:14–18) – a hope that the writer sees as cohering with the message of Paul (3:15b–16).

The central theme of 2 Peter, the parousia, provides the theological context for the narration of the transfiguration account. This story lacks a surprising number of details in comparison with the Synoptic account, such as the presence of Moses and Elijah, Peter's proposal to construct three tents, the names and number of the disciples (apart from Peter), the reference to their fear, and the overshadowing cloud. Perhaps the readers of 2 Peter were already so familiar with the story that they needed only a few details to remind them (see 1:12-15). At the same time, these details are not chosen haphazardly and accord well with the overall theme of the epistle.[5] For the author of 2 Peter, the symbolic details are carefully chosen to encapsulate what is, for him, the very theological essence of the transfiguration.

The narrative is structured in three parts: the introduction that establishes the authenticity of what is to be narrated, the actual account of the transfiguration, and the conclusion which confirms the authenticity of the tradition, on the basis of eyewitness testimony. The result is a very simple inclusion or chiasm, with the first and last sections paralleling each other: see Table 4.1.

Table 4.1

a *Introduction:* *Basis of Parousia* (1:16)	Parousia of Christ based not on fantasy but on eyewitness testimony of transfiguration: *'we made known to you … as eyewitnesses'*	
	b *Narrative of Transfiguration* (1:17)	Jesus receives honour and glory, with Father's voice declaring his identity as Son
a¹ *Conclusion:* *Basis of Transfiguration* (1:18)	Transfiguration of Christ based on experience of eyewitnesses: *'we heard … we were with him'*	

From a technical point of view, the main critical issue is the relationship of this story to the other New Testament accounts of the transfiguration. On the one hand, it is possible that the story has its origins in one or other of the Synoptic Gospels which our author has used, making editorial changes to suit his own purposes. The most likely candidate is the Gospel of Matthew, which is closest to the version in 2 Peter.[6] On the other hand, the story may have no direct relationship to the Synoptic Gospels, but may come from an independent tradition, perhaps with its ultimate source in Peter himself.[7] This latter view could account for the insistence on the eyewitness nature of this event; on the other hand, the notion of eyewitness in the literature of the New Testament is notoriously difficult to pin down.[8] The word for eyewitness in 2 Peter (*epoptai*, 1:16) is also used of initiates in the Hellenistic mystery religions, suggesting a more mystical meaning than the forensic implications we normally associate with the word.[9] In the end, it is impossible to be sure of the source of the story in 2 Peter. It is not necessary to assume a literary dependence on Matthew or any of the Synoptic Gospels – the differences are considerable. Evidence from John's Gospel, indefinite though it may be, suggests (as we will see in the next chapter) that the story of the transfiguration was already widely known in the New Testament world, and may even have served as a basis for the authority of the three apostles.[10]

The story of the transfiguration is introduced with a polemical note, confirming the truth of the parousia which the author's opponents deny. This central tenet of Christian teaching, which is part of the core of apostolic faith in this epistle, is not, according to 2 Peter, based on fabrications and myths. It seems odd at first to find the word 'myth' used in a very modern (if debased) sense in the ancient world, as if it meant something that is by definition untrue. Yet, for Jews and Christians, the mythological structures of the pagan world, with their dependence on polytheism and pantheism, supported a false view of the divine, a diversion from worship of the one, true God. The author of 2 Peter is not arguing here against myth in itself. More likely, he is using the language of his opponents against them: they are the ones who teach that Christ's future coming is a 'myth', in the worst sense (see 1 Tim. 1:4; 4:7; 2 Tim. 4:4; Titus 1:14). The key here is the adjectival phrase 'not with cleverly contrived' myths. For the opponents, the parousia is an invention, uninspired by the Spirit and composed for the purpose of controlling Christian behaviour with the promise of rewards and with the threat of punishment on the day of judgement.[11]

As readers, we are not surprised that our author should attempt to defend himself against the charge of fabricating truth. Two things are unexpected, however, about his defence.[12] In the first place, he shifts from the first person singular – which he has employed several times in the previous section (1:12–15) – to the first person plural: now he speaks of 'we' in place of 'I', addressing his audience as the representative of a group. The context shows that this group refers to the apostles who have witnessed the transfiguration, among whom is the implied author (Peter). The shift from singular to plural, from the concerns of an individual Church leader to the common traditions of the apostolic community, introduces a solemn note. What the readers are to remember above all else is precisely the apostolic testimony – a testimony couched in formal and dignified language – since what 2 Peter has to say stands at the heart of

Christian faith. As eyewitnesses, the apostles are guarantors of the truth of the transfiguration and initiates into its true meaning, a meaning that will only become fully apparent with Christ's return.

The second surprising element is that the author, in wishing to establish the verity and certainty of the parousia – which he refers to in the unusual phrase 'the power and coming (parousia) of our Lord Jesus Christ'[13] – should use the tradition of the transfiguration to do so. We have already seen that the Synoptic transfiguration is both an epiphany and an apocalyptic vision. For the author of 2 Peter, it is the apocalyptic note that dominates, though not without elements that suggest epiphany.[14] There is, in other words, a direct connection between the transfiguration and the parousia in 2 Peter, since both display the one power of God.[15] This power is the power of salvation manifest in Christ but with a strongly future orientation. And just as there is one divine power, so there is one divine advent, distended across time, stretching back from the future into the present.

The narrative of the transfiguration is told in succinct language in the following verse, providing a brief, theological commentary on a familiar story, with its well-known symbols (1:17). The terminology is the writer's own: the verb 'transfigure' does not occur, but instead Jesus receives 'honour and glory' (*timên kai doxan*) from the Father, the equivalent of Mark's 'and he was metamorphosed' (Mark 9:2) or Luke's 'the appearance of his face became changed' (Luke 9:29). Due to the brevity of the narration, nothing is said of Jesus' face or clothing being altered nor is there any reference to the symbol of light at this point, although the glory Jesus obtains, with its overtones of the *Shekinah*, is closely allied to light (see 1:19). Elsewhere in 2 Peter, glory and virtue belong to Jesus (1:3) and the doxology at the end of the epistle ascribes glory to him (3:18). 'Honour' is synonymous though not identical with glory. As an important symbol in the ancient world, honour denotes the tangible and public realization of a person's true value, status and achievements – 'a claim to worth along with the social acknowledgment of worth'.[16] It is clearer here than in the Synoptics that God is the author of the transfiguration, establishing Christ's honour publicly in his role as eschatological ruler and judge.[17]

The transfiguration in 2 Peter is paralleled by the interpretative voice, as also in the Synoptics – though without the intervening details of Moses and Elijah, and Peter's suggestion of three tents.[18] The epistle is more explicit in identifying the voice as that of God. It also associates Jesus with God in the use of parallel wording: God is described by circumlocution as 'the majestic glory' (*megaloprepes*, 1:17), the adjective 'majestic' or 'excellent' having the same root as 'greatness' which is used of Christ in the previous verse (*megaleiotêtos*, 1:16). Though there is no mention of the cloud, the voice addresses Jesus in the hearing of the apostles. The unusual verb 'conveyed' suggests here and in the next verse that the Spirit is the channel of communication just as, in the Synoptics, there is a link between the cloud and the Spirit. The word order puts the emphasis on Jesus as the Son, giving prominence to the Father–Son imagery. With the repetition of 'my', the adjective 'beloved' becomes virtually a title in its own right:[19] 'My Son, my Beloved, this is, in whom I am well pleased.'[20] The wording is almost identical to the Synoptic transfiguration, but is especially close to Matthew who adds the words 'in whom I am well pleased' (Matt. 3:17; 17:5). The divine utterance in 2 Peter reflects the baptism of Jesus as well as his transfiguration.[21]

There is probably a suggestion of enthronement in the language that 2 Peter uses for the transfiguration. The imagery seems to reflect Psalm 2, an enthronement psalm which commemorates the king's coronation and adoption as son of God: 'You are my son; today I have begotten you' (Ps. 2:7).[22] A further parallel is Psalm 8 where humankind is depicted as being crowned 'with glory and honour' (Ps. 8:6; see Heb. 2:9). Both psalms have enthronement overtones, especially Psalm 2, and it is possible that 2 Peter, under this influence, sees the transfiguration as God's enthronement of Jesus before the apostles, an enthronement to be confirmed at the parousia. Yet the symbolism is allusive rather than definitive and should not be pressed. The motif of enthronement is one aspect of the symbolic overtones of the transfiguration, alongside the revelation of divine glory and majesty. Jesus is not literally crowned king on the mount of transfiguration – though his glory reflects divine majesty and sovereignty. The final revelation of Christ enthroned as judge, exercising the divine sovereignty, is eschatological: anticipated here on the mountain but adjourned until the end time.

Jesus' sonship occurs only here in this epistle. Normally, 2 Peter prefers to speak of Jesus as 'Lord' (*kyrios*) and 'Christ' (e.g. 1:2, 8, 14), but also several times as Saviour (*sôtêr*), the three titles being found together in key places (1:11; 2:20; 3:2, 18); at one point, Jesus is referred to as 'the Master who bought them' (*despotes*, 2:1). Moreover, at the beginning of the epistle Jesus is referred to as 'our God and Saviour Jesus Christ' (1:1), with a reference soon after to his 'divine power' (1:3).[23] In conjunction with the use of 'Lord' for both Jesus and God (3:8–10), the symbolism suggests that 2 Peter has a high Christology.[24] The transfiguration becomes 'the expression of Jesus' divine glory' as well as 'the anticipation of his glorious return at the *parousia*'.[25] It has, in other words, the suggestion of an epiphany as well as being primarily an apocalyptic anticipation of the end time.

Despite the smoothness of modern translations, there is no main verb in verse 17, giving the impression that the narration of the transfiguration, though central, is not the main theological point. Rather, the story serves to illustrate the reliability of the apostolic witness to the certainty of the parousia. It is as if verse 17 acts as the preliminary for the main verb that dominates the next verse: 'we ourselves heard'. Here the reference to the voice 'conveyed from heaven' is reiterated, but with the focus on the hearing of Jesus' companions. It is also the first reference to the mountain, confirming (if there was any doubt) that the author is narrating the transfiguration story. The description of the mountain as 'holy' refers not to any specific location in the Old Testament (e.g. Mount Sinai or Mount Sion) but rather to the transfiguration itself, which makes the place holy. As in the Synoptics, the mountain setting stresses the nearness to heaven and the sense of a boundary location between earth and heaven.

In the verses following this section (1:19–21), the author speaks of the power and reliability of the prophetic word which is 'like a lamp shining in a gloomy place' or like the dawning of the day or like the rising of the star that heralds the morning (1:19). The language of light, traditionally associated with the transfiguration, provides a bridge to the theme of prophecy. Indeed, the close connection suggests that the transfiguration itself belongs within the realm of 'prophecy'.[26] Later in the epistle, 2 Peter equates the teaching of the 'holy prophets' with the teachings of Christ 'through your apostles' (3:2). The wider context of this discussion is Christian belief in the parousia, the future return of Christ on the 'day of the Lord' (3:10). Just as God created the heavens and earth through the divine word, so they will come to an end and God will create a new heaven and earth (3:5–7, 13). Because the apostles have been witnesses of Christ's majesty on the mountain, their prophecy of his parousia (unlike the denial of the false prophets and teachers, 2:1; 3:3–4) is credible and authentic. It too is grounded in the word of God, the same voice that spoke on the holy mountain confirming Jesus' identity. The story of the transfiguration and its true meaning has its source in the Holy Spirit, therefore, who inspires both the prophetic voice and the apostolic teaching (3:21). It is not insignificant that the same verb used here of the Spirit's inspiring is also used of the voice at the transfiguration (*pherein*, 1:17–18, 21).

What, then, is the theological relationship between the transfiguration and the parousia in 2 Peter? The simplest answer is that the one acts as an anticipation of the other. The transfiguration is a foretaste of the power of Jesus to be revealed in the fulfilment of God's reign. The transfiguration thus serves as the guarantor of the parousia. Because the apostles have already witnessed Jesus in his 'greatness', the reader can be sure that this majesty will again manifest itself in God's eschatological reign or kingdom. The one guarantees the certainty of the other. Normally we might expect the resurrection to be given this anticipatory role, pledging the reality of God's future in accord with the presence of the Spirit.[27] But in 2 Peter it is the transfiguration that is given the function of anticipating the final appearance of Christ. This is in itself extraordinary and bestows upon the transfiguration a remarkably high status. The metamorphosis of Jesus – the revelation of his 'glory and honour' – is located before his death at the heart of his ministry, with definitive eschatological consequences.

Yet there is more to it than that. The transfiguration is not a 'sneak preview' of that which does not yet exist, any more than elsewhere in the New Testament the resurrection is – except in relation to the destiny of all creation (Rom. 8:19). What is disclosed at the transfiguration is Jesus' true identity as Son, whose appearance on the mountain stands symbolically, in our author's mind, for the incarnation and the resurrection. The argument is not simply that Jesus appeared once in an anticipatory way and therefore will appear again at the dismantling and remaking of the world. Rather, the anticipatory appearance is of the one who is none other than the divine Son, the Beloved, whose sublime identity is itself the pledge of God's promise. Thus everything in this brief story serves to bolster the message ('prophecy') of the parousia, grounded in Jesus' identity: the manifestation of 'glory and honour', the voice from heaven, the identification of the Son, and the presence of the apostolic eyewitnesses and initiates whose testimony, based on the inspiration of the Holy Spirit, is firmly to be trusted. Alongside the strongly apocalyptic thrust of the transfiguration in 2 Peter is an epiphanic note: the certainty of the future is based on the identity of Jesus, already manifest in the present on the holy mountain.

One further point remains. 2 Peter is concerned not simply to teach the reliability of the parousia tradition, but also to encourage the readers to re-shape their lives in accordance with that hope and expectation. The qualities of Christian living that the author calls for are set out at the beginning and end of the epistle (1:5–11; 3:11–12, 14–18). Although there is no usage of the word 'transfiguration', either in relation to Christ or believers, the epistle does speak of Christians becoming 'sharers in the divine nature' (*theias koinônoi physeôs*, 1:4). The eschatological remaking of creation includes the remaking of believers whose destiny is to participate in the very nature of God, a participation that is made possible only through the appearing of the Beloved, both on the holy mountain and at the end. Salvation, for 2 Peter, is incomplete until the end, until the final coming of Christ as both Lord and Saviour. The transfiguration, which embodies symbolically the first coming of Christ, is thus the surety of the participation of believers in the divine life. The apostolic witnesses look to this hope and encourage their converts to do likewise. For Christians too there will be a revelation that displays their 'honour and glory', with a voice declaring them to be the children of God; for this reason, they too are already called 'beloved' in the epistle (3:1, 14, 17). Their task is to 'expect and hasten towards' the parousia, knowing that it is the place of transfiguration, the re-creation of a world 'in which righteousness will dwell' (3:12–13). Through the transfiguration, the destiny of believers is to share in the nature and glory of God.

The narrative in 2 Peter uses the transfiguration in a way that parallels, though is not identical to, the Synoptic accounts, adapting the same basic story to the author's own theological intent. Two points, in particular, stand out in this 'Petrine' re-telling of the tale. First, through its succinct narration and the omission of some details (as it happens, the more problematical ones), the transfiguration in 2 Peter is focused much more sharply on the parousia. It becomes symbolic of the first coming of the Lord, as that coming makes way for and guarantees the second. This focus on the parousia stresses the centrality of the transfiguration in the ministry of Jesus. The transfiguration is not an incidental occurrence, in this view, but integral to the story of Jesus – so much so that it is able, in some sense, to encapsulate symbolically the incarnation. Its function as a precursor to and pledge of the parousia gives it a distinctly saving role within the theological framework of the epistle.

Second, the tradition of the transfiguration also establishes the apostolic credentials. By being placed alongside the Old Testament witness, the transfiguration ensures that prophets and apostles together, through the agency of the Holy Spirit, declare the one word of God, the word of salvation to be revealed on the 'day of God' (3:12). Here 2 Peter identifies the transfiguration as a non-negotiable part of apostolic faith, central to its evangelical message. The transfiguration lies at the core of the apostolic tradition, inspiring hope in the return of Christ and God's final redemption. Although that day will come suddenly, like a thief in the night, it will be like the advent of the dawn, radiant with light and glory. Christians are called to live between the appearance of Christ on the holy mountain and his appearance at the end. Living between these two events – which represent the one divine advent – and in full awareness of their truth means that believers are transfigured, participating more and more in the divine nature as revealed in Christ.

Notes

1 See Martin, R. P., 'The Theology of Jude, 1 Peter and 2 Peter', in Martin, R. P. and Chester, A. (eds), *The Theology of the Letters of James, Peter, and Jude*, Cambridge University Press, Cambridge, 1994, 139–40.

2 There is a common tradition within Judaism of pseudonymous writings, e.g. the large body of wisdom literature of the Old Testament and beyond, all of which claims to go back to Solomon.

3 Reicke, B., *The Epistles of James, Peter, and Jude, Translated with an Introduction and Notes*, Doubleday, New York, 1964, 143–7, and Bauckham, R., *Jude, 2 Peter*, Word Books, Waco, TX, 1986, 210. There is also a close relationship between 2 Peter and Jude, the latter probably influencing the former; see Harrington, D. J., 'Jude and 2 Peter', in Senior, D. P. and Harrington, D. J. (eds), *1 Peter, Jude and 2 Peter*, Liturgical Press, Collegeville, MN, 2003, 162–4.

4 See Moses, A. D. A., *Matthew's Transfiguration Story and Jewish–Christian Controversy* (ed. S. E. Porter), Sheffield Academic Press, Sheffield, 1996, 211.

5 Bauckham, *Jude, 2 Peter*, 210, and Miller, R. D., 'Is There Independent Attestation for the Transfiguration in 2 Peter?' *New Testament Studies* 50, 1996, 620–1.

6 So Miller, 'Transfiguration in 2 Peter', 620–5.

7 Bauckham, *Jude, 2 Peter*, 205–12, and Kelly, J. N. D., *A Commentary on the Epistles of Peter and of Jude* (ed. H. Chadwick), A. & C. Black, London, 1969, 319; also Best, E., 'The Markan Redaction of the Transfiguration', in Livingstone, E. A. (ed.), *International Congress on Biblical Studies*, Akademie, Berlin, 1982, 42.

8 See, for example, the witness of the beloved disciple in the Gospel of John where it is unclear whether it is eyewitness testimony or

theological interpretation that is in mind (John 19:35; 20:24).

9 Ramsay, M., *The Glory of God and the Transfiguration of Christ*, 2nd edn, Darton, Longman & Todd, London, 1967, 125, and Bauckham, *Jude, 2 Peter*, 215–16.

10 Further on this, see Wenham, D. and Moses, A. D. A., '"There Are Some Standing Here …": Did They Become the "Reputed Pillars" of the Jerusalem Church? Some Reflections on Mark 9:1, Galatians 2:9 and the Transfiguration', *Novum Testamentum* 36, 1994, 146–63. It may be that James the son of Zebedee was replaced at some stage by James the Just to form the three 'pillars' of the earliest community (Gal. 2:9).

11 Perkins, P., *First and Second Peter, James, and Jude*, John Knox, Louisville, KY, 1995, 173–4.

12 Note that Peter is defending not his own authority as an apostle but rather the apostolic teaching of the parousia; Bauckham, *Jude, 2 Peter*, 216, 221–2.

13 The phrase 'power and parousia' really has the sense of 'the power of his parousia' or 'his coming in power'; see *ibid.*, 215.

14 Against this, cf. *ibid.*, 215, 217–18. Because he interprets the idea of epiphany as Hellenistic and ignores the biblical notion, Bauckham dismisses it here. Neyrey, J., *2 Peter, Jude: A New Translation with Introduction and Commentary* AB 37c, Doubleday, New York, 1993, 172–4, however, sees the transfiguration in 2 Peter as a theophany.

15 So Boobyer, G. H., *St. Mark and the Transfiguration Story*, T. & T. Clark, Edinburgh, 1942, 43–6.

16 Malina, B. J., *The New Testament World: Insights from Cultural Anthropology*, SCM, London, 1981, 27; also 25–50. See especially Neyrey, *op. cit.*, 172.

17 Bauckham, *Jude, 2 Peter*, 207, 218–22.

18 Why is nothing said of the apostles' misunderstanding at the transfiguration? It is possible that the author feels it could undermine the authority of Peter. On the other hand, in view of the resurrection, such misunderstanding is clearly a thing of the past and irrelevant here.

19 So Bauckham, *Jude, 2 Peter*, 207–9, 220; against this, cf. Miller, 'Transfiguration in 2 Peter', 623.

20 This is probably the original word order of 2 Peter, despite the traditional Matthæan order in a large number of manuscripts; see Metzger, B. M., *A Textual Commentary on the Greek New Testament*, 2nd edn, United Bible Societies, London, 1975, 700–1.

21 There may also be an allusion to the sacrifice of Isaac: in the Greek Old Testament God tells Abraham to take 'your beloved son whom you love' (Gen. 22:2 LXX).

22 See especially Bauckham, *Jude, 2 Peter*, 219–20, who nonetheless argues that there is no adoptionism in 2 Peter's use of the psalm.

23 There is a textual issue here, but as the more difficult reading 'God' is likely to be original – although 'God' and 'Saviour' could refer, respectively, to God and Jesus. See Martin, *op. cit.*, 159.

24 Danker, E. W., '2 Peter', in Krodel, G. (ed.), *The General Letters: Hebrews, James, 1–2 Peter, Jude, 1–2–3 John*, Fortress, Minneapolis, MN, 1995, 87–92.

25 Harrington, 'Jude and 2 Peter', 256.

26 Neyrey, *op. cit.*, 169–70.

27 Kelly, *op. cit.*, 320.

5
Transfiguration in John and Elsewhere in the New Testament

In addition to the Synoptic Gospels and 2 Peter, transfiguration themes and imagery are to be found elsewhere in the New Testament. Their presence suggests, indeed, that the transfiguration story – perhaps in different forms – was widespread in the early Church and not simply a Markan invention. Admittedly, this is not an easy point to establish, since transfiguration symbols have their background in Old Testament imagery that is common to the New Testament writers. However, where there is a congruence of symbols, especially those associated with light, glory and revelation, we may detect echoes, if not actual knowledge, of the transfiguration story. This is particularly the case with the Gospel of John, the whole of which can be viewed as a 'transfiguration' narrative. But there are also traces in other parts of the New Testament too: in the letters of Paul, for example, in the Apocalypse, and also elsewhere. In each case, the symbols present Jesus as God's gracious self-revelation, a revelation that shimmers with light, beauty and glory.

Despite the divergences, the Synoptic Gospels and 2 Peter each view the transfiguration as central to the message of the gospel, inextricably bound up with Jesus' identity as the divine Son; with his death and resurrection (especially the Synoptics); and with the future glory of his parousia (2 Peter). Each displays the integration of apocalyptic vision and epiphany, the present status and the future destiny, revealing a hidden identity and an eschatological exaltation that dazzles those who witness it. From this perspective, it is strange indeed that the same narrative, with its wealth of symbolism, is absent from the Gospel of John. The theme of glory is central to the Fourth Gospel, even more than the Synoptics, running through the narrative from the incarnation, to Jesus' ministry, to his climactic death on the cross. Glory is the beginning and end of John's message, the inner meaning of Jesus' life and death. Why then is the transfiguration story, so commensurate with John's theology in every way, absent from the Fourth Gospel? At first glance, the omission seems inexplicable.

Admittedly, there are a number of stories missing from John's Gospel to which we could well pose a similar question. Yet the transfiguration seems more peculiar in its absence than perhaps any other of the Synoptic stories.

The easiest explanation is that the writer of the Fourth Gospel never actually knew the transfiguration story. In that case, its apparent consonance with the Gospel's symbolic universe is coincidental, stemming from common usage of the Old Testament. If, however, there is any indication that John knew the Synoptic Gospels or (more likely) the traditions on which they are based, the question persists. The issue of the relationship between John and the Synoptics is a complex and long-standing one, observed by readers in the ancient world long before the advent of biblical criticism. No one doubts that the two represent significantly different traditions – the Synoptic and the Johannine – that are not easily harmonized without damage to the integrity of each. If a consensus exists among modern commentators, it is the qualified view that John is largely, though not entirely, independent of the Synoptic Gospels.[1] Given that the category of dependence and independence forms a spectrum, many readers would concede that there are significant points of convergence between the two traditions, convergences that suggest that John, even if he had not read Mark, was aware of similar traditions. The possibility of an independent transfiguration story in 2 Peter suggests that the narrative – in some form or another – had already circulated widely.[2]

If there is cross-fertilization between the two traditions, the Synoptic and the Johannine, the question of why John did not use the transfiguration story becomes more insistent. And here an answer can be suggested: that John did know something of the transfiguration and chose to use it, not as a single tale, but as a motif – a series of symbols – throughout his Gospel. If so, this would mean that, instead of re-telling the story with his own editorial changes, John has chosen to weave the threads of the transfiguration into the warp and woof of his tale, so that the main symbols are rehearsed again and again throughout the Johannine narrative.[3] If so, the whole of the Gospel could be viewed as a 'transfiguration' story:[4] 'the glory which in the Synoptics flashes into the story on the mountain is perceived by Saint John to pervade all the words and works of Jesus.'[5] This Gospel has elements of both epiphany and apocalyptic vision, even though Johannine eschatology is much more radically anticipated in the present than the other Gospels. In whatever guise and however modified, epiphany and apocalyptic vision are pressed into the service of John's unique theology.

If this supposition is correct, there are a number of transfiguration elements we might expect to find, in some form or another, in the Johannine recasting of the story. These elements should involve some, at least, of the following:

- the geographical features: the mountain, the light and the cloud;
- the presence of Moses and Elijah;
- the change in bodily form to reveal Jesus' glory;
- the reference to tents;
- the voice of God, confirming Jesus as the divine Son, and directing the disciples to listen to his teaching;
- the presence of disciples, their fear, incomprehension, and faith.[6]

There are a number of passages in John's Gospel that contain these elements, yet their usage is carefully edited. While it is possible to debate the choice of passages, arguing that aspects of the transfiguration are ubiquitous in the Fourth Gospel, several incidents stand out for particular attention:[7]

And the Word become flesh and dwelt among us. And we beheld his glory, the glory of the Father's only Son, full of grace and truth. (John 1:14)

Jesus did this, the first of the signs, in Cana of Galilee and he revealed his glory and his disciples believed in him. (John 2:11)

Jesus went up the mountain and there he sat down with his disciples. ... 11 Jesus then took the loaves and having given thanks he distributed them to those reclining and likewise also the fish, as much as they wanted. ... 35 Jesus said to them, 'I am the bread of life; the one coming to me will never hunger and the one believing in me will never thirst.' (John 6:3, 11, 35)

27 'Now my soul is troubled and what am I to say? Father, save me from this hour? But for this purpose I have come, for this hour. 28 Father, glorify your name.' Then a voice came from heaven: 'Indeed, I have glorified it and I will glorify it again.' (John 12:27–8)

Jesus said these things and having raised his eyes to heaven he said, 'Father, the hour has come. Glorify your Son, so that the Son may glorify you.' (John 17:1)

The Prologue sets the scene for John's Gospel like a musical overture, capturing many of the themes and symbols that are to come (1:1–18).[8] The symbolism of light is strong, associated indirectly with John the Baptist and directly with the coming of the Word (*Logos*), the one through whom the light of creation first dawned (1:4–9; Gen. 1:3). As there is no explicit topography, the imagery of the mountain and the cloud – symbols of divine presence – is absent, but the heightened language conveys a similar impression of lofty transcendence and mystery; as if the reader is caught up into the heights, on the boundary between heaven and earth. The Prologue is an example of 'barrier penetration', the crossing of boundaries in which the heavenly world opens its gates to disclose light and life.[9] Although there is no mention of Elijah in the Prologue, John speaks explicitly of Moses as the source and giver of the law (1:17), who points to the 'grace and truth' in Jesus: not in opposition but complementary, the one paving the way for and making possible the other.[10]

Transfiguration language becomes explicit at the turning-point of the Prologue (1:14),[11] where John introduces the incarnation, the advent of the Word in flesh.[12] As Jesus is transfigured in the other Gospels to reveal his true identity, so in the Prologue Jesus' flesh manifests divine glory. For John, the term 'flesh' (*sarx*) is different from its adverse Pauline usage.[13] In the Fourth Gospel, by contrast, flesh is not negative; though ineffective of itself to procure salvation (1:13; 6:63), it is not necessarily evil or inimical to God. Indeed, the flesh of the divine Word becomes a major symbol of salvation, being a form of metonymy, encapsulating the whole person of Jesus, body and soul. In that flesh, Jesus reveals his identity as the divine Word and Son, the one who exists in intimate union with the Father.[14] The transfigured flesh of Jesus reflects God's life-giving glory.[15] While there is no explicit mention of the divine voice speaking in the Prologue, God 'speaks' the definitive divine utterance in Jesus. The voice of the Father utters the one Word in the Son, resonating through eternity (1:1–2, 18).

This verse contains the first reference to glory in the Fourth Gospel. Throughout the Gospel, John will use glory in its Old Testament sense to signify the radiant presence of God with Israel, a presence that is both loving and life-giving. Glory is a central Johannine theme, found in the

Gospel either as a noun, 'glory' (*doxa*),[16] or in its verbal form 'to glorify' (*doxazein*).[17] This glory is profoundly christological: in his flesh Jesus is the revelation of divine glory because the same radiance – the majestic yet intimate presence that is a major characteristic of the transfiguration – is revealed in him. The Johannine Jesus participates fully in the divine realm and divine being: '*doxa*, for John, means nothing other than Jesus' divinity.'[18]

There is a parallel here with the tabernacle in the wilderness which, as the dwelling-place of God's glory, prefigures the Word dwelling among human beings. The verb 'dwelt' means literally 'pitched his tent' (*eskênôsen*, from the noun *skênê* meaning 'tent'). The incarnation parallels the temple on Mount Sion, the 'mountain of God' (Ps. 25:8; Wis. 7:25, 9:8–11; Sir. 24:8), corresponding to Peter's desire in the Synoptic Gospels to build three tents (Mark 9:5–6). God's presence, in John, abides in the sacred tent or temple which is Jesus himself. Peter's inappropriate proposal is thus changed in John to become the one divine 'Tent' in which/whom the Father's presence abides. The mountain symbolism is implicit in the language. This will become clearer in the story of the Samaritan woman, a passage that draws on 1:14 for its imagery. True worship of the Father is centred now on Jesus as the place of God's dwelling, and not on geographical locations such as holy mountains (4:16–26): 'neither on this mountain nor in Jerusalem' (4:21). The 'mountain of God' and the true 'tent' are symbols of the Johannine Jesus.

Jesus' identity is essential for John's understanding of faith and salvation. The 'we' at 1:14 refers to the community of faith, those who have received new birth from God (1:12–13; see 3:1–8) and who now belong intimately to the divine realm. The same 'we' is found in 2 Peter in the account of the transfiguration, where the apostles 'heard from heaven' the voice acclaiming Jesus as Son and Beloved (2 Pet. 1:18).[19] And just as the disciples in the Synoptic Gospels see Jesus' metamorphosis and hear the divine voice, so in John there is a seeing and a hearing for the disciples. They too 'behold the glory', but the sight and the hearing are one: to see Jesus is simultaneously to hear the voice of God, since he is the Word incarnate, the voice of God from before creation. Believers come to share in the divine nature, just as – and indeed solely because – the Word comes to share in human nature (1:12).

There is an important difference in John's understanding of transfiguration at this point, alongside the remarkable symbolic similarities. In the other Gospels, Jesus is changed from an ordinary humanity that veils his identity to a transcendent humanity that radiates divine presence. In the Prologue, the metamorphosis seems almost the opposite: from spirit to flesh, from divine to human, from a transcendent divinity, the source of all life (1:3–4), to a divinity that shows itself in the material world, face to face. Gregory of Nazianzus speaks of the incarnation as an act of divine condescension and self-emptying:

> The one who is, becomes. The uncreated is created ... The one who enriches becomes a beggar; for he begs for my own flesh, so that I might become rich in his divinity. The one who is full becomes empty; for he empties himself of his glory for a little time so that I might share in his fullness ... I received the image (*eikôn*) and I did not protect it; he received a share in my flesh so that he might even save the image and make deathless the flesh.[20]

Here the divine being enters the material world with transforming power, shaped by flesh that becomes symbolic of God's indwelling. Jesus in this Gospel is the epiphany of God's presence. To gaze into the face of Jesus is to see, simultaneously, the Father's glory and the restoration of humanity, since Christ is 'the foundational symbol, the very revelation of God'.[21] This revelation is not confined to occasional moments of epiphany, where Jesus' true identity bursts from its earthly bounds, but is present in every contour of his life and being. For the believer, there is no hiddenness to the revelation, no cloud to hide it from sight. John's use of the transfiguration tradition shifts its focus from the mid-point of Jesus' ministry to the incarnation in general, where what is primarily 'transfigured' is God, fashioned in mortal flesh. As a result, to the eyes of faith ('we beheld'), Jesus' flesh is a perpetual metamorphosis of God's glory.

The second passage that contains echoes of the transfiguration is the Wedding at Cana (2:1–11). Absent are the geographical references and any overt mention of Moses or Elijah. Nonetheless, the jars of purification, representing the religion and rites of Judaism, play a similar role to Moses and Elijah. They point to Jesus as the newness of revelation, a revelation that emerges from the structures of the old. As the first of Jesus' signs in the Gospel, the clues to this story are found in the references to the 'hour' and glory. Speaking of his glorification on the cross, Jesus informs his mother that his hour 'has not yet come' (2:4; 12:23; 13:1), an hour when she will play a vital part in the birth of the new community (19:25–7). John concludes with an overt reference to glory: 'and he revealed his glory and his disciples believed in him' (2:11). The epiphany of glory is the purpose of the Cana miracle and indeed the purpose of Jesus' entire life and death. It is neither hidden nor momentary in its manifestation to the disciples. Alongside the notion of Jesus' 'hour' and the revealing of God's glory is the theme of faith in the efficacious word of Jesus. Note the parallel here with the divine voice in the Synoptic transfiguration. From within the cloud, God summons the three disciples to 'listen to him' (Mark 9:7), directing their attention to Jesus' teaching on the journey to Jerusalem. In John's Gospel, the instructions of the mother of Jesus to the stewards, which demonstrate remarkable faith in Jesus and 'the efficacy of his word',[22] form a kind of parallel to the heavenly voice from the cloud (2:5). Just as the Synoptic disciples are told to listen to the words of Jesus, so the Johannine disciples hear the instruction to the stewards to do whatever Jesus, the Word of God, commands.

Yet the wedding at Cana does involve a kind of 'transfiguration', though not a physical change in Jesus himself. John draws a contrast between Jewish traditions (which form the backbone to the Gospel), symbolized in the water, and the advent of Jesus which is the symbolic meaning of the wine. His coming effects the transfiguration of Judaism: from a lesser to a greater revelation, from 'signs and shadows' to their full reality.[23] At the heart of this 'transfiguration' is the unfolding of a glory that, for John, is veiled in Israel's past – although recognized by Abraham, Moses and Isaiah – but now unveiled in the person of Jesus. In the change of water into wine, it is Judaism that is transfigured at Cana. The rituals and feasts of Judaism become the symbolic medium that take the reader to Jesus, the incarnate Son of God. As the identity of Jesus is revealed in splendour on the mountain in the Synoptic transfiguration through the change in his bodily form, so in the Johannine story the glory of Jesus is revealed at the wedding at Cana through the changing of water into wine.

The third Johannine story that suggests the influence of the transfiguration is the Bread of Life narrative in John 6.[24] In this story, Jesus feeds a large crowd with a very small quantity of food – five barley loaves and two small fish (6:9). Afterwards the people pursue Jesus, wanting to make him king (6:15); in typically Johannine fashion, they misunderstand the feeding and interpret it on a material or literal level, as food to fill their bellies. Jesus draws them towards a spiritual and symbolic understanding of what has occurred: not the food that perishes but the food that 'abides to eternal life' (6:27). At first, the crowds seem open to Jesus' words but they become increasingly alienated from his teaching, including those among the wider group of disciples (6:60).

The language of glory is implicit rather than explicit in this Johannine story. Even so, characteristic transfiguration elements are present. This time the setting for the sign is a mountain in an unspecified location in Galilee (6:3).[25] The loaves and fish are not changed into something different, as with the water at Cana, but are multiplied into an astonishing abundance that feeds 5,000 people (6:10) and leaves twelve baskets of scraps (6:12–13). The numinous nature of the 'sign' is underscored by Jesus' epiphany on the water to the frightened disciples immediately after the feeding (6:16–21). It develops in the symbolic meaning that the feeding takes on during the dialogue that follows (6:22–65). Throughout the story, even amid misunderstanding and hostility, John presents Jesus as the true 'bread which has come down from heaven' (6:33, 41, 50–1). Jesus acts as both the giver of the bread and also the heavenly food – the host and the repast in one (6:53–8).[26]

Parallels with the transfiguration are apparent in the references to Moses and the exodus imagery. The feeding takes place near Passover (6:4), Jesus' explanation reminds the people of the manna from heaven (6:31–3), the ancestors of Israel in the wilderness are alluded to several times (6:31, 49, 58), and the rebellious mutterings of 'the Jews' echo the complaining Israelites, most of whom never enter the Promised Land (6:41–3; Exod. 16:2–3, 6–9, 12). Even the divine voice is present in Jesus' testimony to the Father. For John, it is the voice of God that 'speaks' in the transfiguring revelation of Jesus as the Bread of Life. Those who listen to Jesus are hearing the Father's voice, since Jesus is the Word whose teaching is divine in origin: 'everyone who hears and learns from the Father comes to me' (6:45). The faith of the disciples is also an important theme, creating a sharp division that is characteristic of John's Gospel; at the end when others have left, scandalized by Jesus' words, Peter confesses his faith in Jesus as 'the Holy One of God' (6:67–9). Once again, though the change occurs with the multiplying of the food, what is really revealed is Jesus' identity as the eternal Son made flesh: 'for the bread of God is that which (or the one who) comes down from heaven and gives life to the world' (6:33). Transfiguration themes and motifs are once again present, articulating symbolically the revelation of divine glory in the person and work of Jesus.

The fourth passage that has links to the transfiguration is the coming of the Greeks (12:20–36). Their sudden approach to two of Jesus' disciples has an extraordinary effect on Jesus, signalling that at last the 'hour' of his departure has come. Now, in the words of the hostile Pharisees in the preceding passage, 'the world has gone after him' (12:19). There is no overt 'transfiguration' in this story but the 'hour' signals the coming revelation of glory – both Jesus' own and the Father's – in the context of Jesus' death. Jesus possesses divine authority over life and death (5:17–30),[27] and is thus able to 'lay down my life in order that I might take it up again' (10:17–18). In a deeper sense, the Greeks are not bypassed but shown that to 'see' Jesus means believing in him as the revelation of God. They are called to serve and follow as he makes his journey through death to life (12:24–6).[28]

None of this would seem particularly reflective of the transfiguration were it not for the ensuing verses. Here John weaves together elements that are familiar from the transfiguration and Gethsemane stories in the Synoptic tradition (12:27–33; Mark 14:32–42).[29] The Jesus of John's Gospel, unlike the Synoptic Jesus, though tempted, chooses not to pray for the removal of the cup despite his distress; instead his prayer is that the Father's name be glorified (12:28; cf. Mark 14:36/Matt. 26:39/Luke 22:42). While this prayer is surely the Johannine equivalent of the Synoptic 'thy will be done', John places great stress on the unbroken unity of will between Father and Son. More importantly, this is the only place in the Gospel where the Father, in response to Jesus' prayer, speaks directly: 'I have glorified it and I will glorify it again' (12:28). Just as the voice of God from the cloud at the Synoptic transfiguration confirms Jesus' identity at the beginning of his journey to suffering and death, so the voice of the Johannine Father confirms the 'hour' of the passion as the moment of glorification. And as in the Synoptic Gospels, God's voice speaks not for the benefit of Jesus but for those present (John 12:30; see 11:42), who will witness Jesus' exaltation on the cross when he draws 'all people' – or 'all things' – to himself (12:32).[30]

Using the imagery of light, Jesus challenges the crowd to believe in the face of their misunderstanding (12:29). As a major symbol of the Fourth Gospel, light is a manifestation of God's glory (12:35–6; see 1:3–5). Already in the Gospel narrative, the evangelist has linked the symbol of light with the feast of Tabernacles,[31] where Jesus speaks as the Light of the world (8:12; 9:5). The imagery parallels the whiteness/light symbolism of the transfiguration story. The dazzling light gleaming in the Synoptic Gospels from Jesus' clothes and, in Matthew and Luke, from his face, is a divine light – an unearthly radiance whose source transcends creation. The Johannine Jesus possesses the same divine light. The glory that resides in him is the glory of the *Shekinah*, the heavenly light that the presence of God emits, synonymous with eternal life. The Synoptic Gethsemane scene, which depicts Jesus' (successful) struggle to face death and obey the Father's will, becomes in the hands of the fourth evangelist a moment of transfiguration, revealing Jesus' true identity, his oneness with the Father, and his God-ordained destiny to return to heavenly glory via the cross. The transfiguration elements of this Johannine narrative emerge precisely as the passion begins.[32]

The final illustration of the influence of transfiguration symbols is the prayer of the Johannine Jesus at the end of his long discourse. Together with the footwashing (13:1–35), these two episodes frame the farewell discourse, with the symbolism of the vine at the centre (15:1–17).[33] The prayer of the ascending Redeemer is performative,[34] the symbolic enactment of Jesus' impending glorification on the cross.[35] In John's understanding, the cross is not the low point of Jesus' ministry nor the darkest moment of humiliation and shame, but the high point, a lifting up, a moment of glory and radiance (3:13–15; 12:32, 13:31–2). The Son glorifies the Father by revealing the radical nature of God's love and the Father glorifies the Son by drawing him back into the realm from whence he came. In this prayer the Son is fully present to the Father, 'turned towards God' as at the beginning (1:1–2, 18),[36] revealing the glory which is the meaning of his life and death. He is the true temple in whom the divine glory dwells. While there is no mountain symbolism, the same sense of loftiness and elevation is present. The manifestation of glory is confirmed in the repetition of the language of glory throughout Jesus' prayer: in the opening verses (17:1–5) and towards the end (17:10, 22, 24). What is transfiguring about Jesus' identity is precisely the ascent which the prayer enacts. Just as at 1:14 the metamorphosis consists of the change from Word to flesh, and the revelation of glory in that flesh as a permanent manifestation of the radiance of the Father, so now at the end the metamorphosis lies in Jesus' ascent to God and the fullness of glory, an ascent he makes in the flesh. The cross, like the prayer, represents the ascent of the Son to the Father.

John 17 represents also the gathering of the whole creation into the glory of God, as indicated in the use of 'all flesh' at the beginning of Jesus' prayer (17:2).[37] This ingathering is focused on the community of faith, both present and future, the 'we' of 1:14 being now the subject of the prayer. Unlike the Synoptic Gospels, the disciples do understand at this point (see 16:29–30) and are not terrified at entering the 'cloud' of Jesus' glory[38] – although their subsequent abandonment of Jesus shows the limits of their faith (16:31–2).[39] John emphasizes the unity of the community as it is gathered into the epiphany of God's glory, a glory Jesus shares with his disciples (17:22). His longing that future disciples 'see my glory' (17:24) makes clear that the sight of Jesus in the stance of prayer, his life and death an ascent to the Father, is sufficient. To see him with the eyes of faith is to be transfigured.

The elements of transfiguration present in the prayer of Jesus in John 17 parallel the incarnation at 1:14. Jesus' ascent to the Father, which is the meaning of the passion, is the climax of the manifestation of glory in the Fourth Gospel. It is this glory which the disciples behold on the cross, as they witness the title above Jesus' head, the wholeness of the seamless robe (19:23–4), the founding of the new community around the mother of Jesus and the beloved disciple (19:25–7), the fulfilment of Jesus' desire to do the Father's will (19:28–30a), the bestowal of the Spirit at Jesus' death (19:30b; cf. 20:19–23), and the sacramental flow of blood and water from his side (19:31–7).[40] All these are symbols of glory present in Jesus the divine Son, whose metamorphosis into mortal flesh is the source of life and salvation. Paradoxically, the crucified body of Christ becomes an icon of life and glory.[41] Here the overtones of the transfiguration are remarkably strong, even where the topographical and narrative elements of the Synoptic transfiguration are absent.

Yet while John probably knows and approves of the story of the transfiguration, there are a number of elements he may well have wished to downplay or even avoid. In the first place, he may have disliked the confining of Jesus' glory to one episode, preferring to scatter the story throughout his Gospel, as a consequence of his emphasis on glory. Second, he may have felt that the heavy stress on the future made for a serious limitation in the transfiguration story. Whereas glory in the other Gospels is associated with the future coming of the Son of Man (Mark 13:26), in the Fourth Gospel, as we have seen, that coming is radically anticipated in the incarnation (1:14). There are apocalyptic elements in John, but they are mostly realized in the present,[42] giving rise to what has been called (with some hyperbole) the 'magnificent onesidedness of Johannine eschatology'.[43] As a result, John's use of transfiguration symbolism draws it into the orbit of the incarnation. Third, John may have found the theme of hiddenness confining. In Mark's Gospel, there is a decided secrecy to the revelation (e.g. Mark

1:10; 15:38), yet the disciples are painfully slow in believing. The divine voice enjoins the disciples to 'listen to him' (Mark 9:5), underscoring the disciples' own need of illumination and 'transfiguration'. By contrast, while the disciples in John have moments of incomprehension and are in need of transfiguration, they move more readily to an understanding of Jesus, even though this remains incomplete until Easter. The identity of the Johannine Jesus is more explicit and less hidden (1:6–8, 15, 29–36, 41–51; 2:11). It is certainly not received by everyone, but even those who reject it do so in a way that makes it shine out the more (e.g. 11:47–53). Thus, no single moment of revelation rises above another: everything in John discloses, without reservation, Jesus' divinely human identity. Jesus' enemies stand in no doubt of the nature of his claims. John's understanding of the transfiguration is thus more publicly displayed and more accessible, even on those rare occasions when Jesus withdraws or hides himself (11:54; 12:36). In John's Gospel, Jesus' divine identity is transparent throughout the Gospel, which sees one epiphany folding over into another.

If there is a sense of metamorphosis in John's use of the transfiguration, it lies not in solitary moments but in the incarnation itself, portrayed in Jesus' ministry and his self-sacrificing, God-centred death on the cross. The transfiguration occurs again and again in the self-giving life and love of God which crosses the chasm between divine and human. The very being of God – ineffable, invisible, unknowable, intangible (1:18; 6:46) – stoops to enter the world of speech, sight, perception, hearing, touch; bringing divinity to humanity, immortality to mortality, eternity to time. The effect is that Jesus' flesh possesses a cosmic quality, crossing barriers of space and time. Like Thomas, future believers who depend on his faith (and that of the other 'apostolic' witnesses) stand before the risen Christ, seeing the still-open wounds from which blood and water flow, and acclaim him 'Lord and God' (20:28).[44] The condescension of glory to flesh leads to the metamorphosis of 'all flesh', made and re-made in the image of the Son.

In addition to the Gospel of John, there are several other places in the New Testament which, implicitly or explicitly, use the language and symbols of the transfiguration. The transfiguring of believers as a consequence of Christ's appearing, for example, is found in two different contexts in Paul's epistles. Although there is no reference to the transfiguration story in either passage, Paul uses parallel imagery, the verb 'transfigure' referring to the transformation of Christians into Christ. In the first passage the echoes of the transfiguration are discernible:[45]

3:16 But whenever one turns to the Lord, the veil is removed. 17 Now the Lord is the Spirit; and where the Spirit of the Lord is, there is freedom. 18 And we all with unveiled face beholding as in a mirror the glory of the Lord are being transfigured into the same image from glory to glory, just as from the Lord, the Spirit ... 4:6 Because God is the one who said, 'From darkness light will shine', who has shone in our hearts for the enlightenment of the knowledge of the glory of God in the face of [Jesus] Christ. (2 Cor. 3:16–18; 4:6)

These verses form part of a wider unit in which Paul contrasts his own ministry in the new age with the ministry of Moses in the old (3:7–4:6): the 'ministry of the Spirit' or 'the ministry of justification' as against 'the ministry of death' or the 'ministry of condemnation' (2 Cor. 3:8, 9).[46] Paul focuses on the detail of the veil over Moses' face on his descent from Mount Sinai (Exod. 34:29–35), interpreting the veil as symbolic of the partial nature of the old age and the law that governed it. Indeed, in this reading, Moses' wearing of the veil is a form of protection by God, 'sparing his people the agony of seeing the last of the splendor'.[47] There is no denial that the law has its own glory, a glory given by God (3:7), but the glory of the old, says Paul, was too much for the children of Israel, not because (as in Exod. 34) it was too dazzling and majestic, but because it was destined to fade (3:7, 13). The setting aside of the veil is symbolic of the new age, therefore, because God's glory – though still majestic and terrifying – never fades from the face of Jesus as it did from Moses. And so, Paul argues, as against unbelieving Israel which still hears the Old Testament with veiled heart (3:14–15), Christians can gaze on the glory without dismay, their faces unveiled.[48]

From here Paul moves to the imagery of metamorphosis, the most complex statement being verse 18, with its sense of compactness, symmetry and rhythmic phrasing. The setting aside of the veil in Christ is the source of Christian transformation. In Paul's language, the removing of the veil occurs when, through conversion, the believer turns to the Lord who gives unhindered vision of the glory of God (3:16).[49] The removing of the veil in Christ leads to that freedom which is the Spirit's gift (3:17). Thus, the divine glory revealed in Christ and given in the Spirit can be seen in its true radiance – no longer fading, partial or temporary (3:18a). The new age of the Spirit, unlike the old age under the law, can now deal decisively with sin and death. Indeed, believers are freed from entrapment to the old age with its destructive patterns of sin and death; they are free to minister the gospel with 'great boldness' (3:12). As a consequence, it is possible to gaze at the glory of God and be changed 'from glory to glory' (*apo doxês eis doxan*, 3:18b).[50] The verb used here is the same as in Mark and Matthew for Jesus' transfiguration (*metamorphoumetha*, 3:18; Mark 9:2; Matt. 17:2). Elsewhere, Paul uses different language for the transformation of believers.[51] Indeed, at one point, Paul speaks in a startling phrase of our awaiting the Lord's coming 'who will change (*metaschmatisei*) the body of our humiliation to the likeness of the body of his glory' (Phil. 3:21)[52] – a phrase that, though referring to the future coming of Christ, recalls Jesus' body in the transfiguration as a 'body of glory'. Yet while transfiguration for Paul is largely future, the present tense of the verb in 2 Corinthians shows that the process has already begun. Christian living, symbolized in baptism, means participating in Christ's death in order to share eschatologically in his resurrection. To witness the glory of God produces the fruits of the Spirit: 'love, joy, peace, patience, kindness, generosity, faithfulness, gentleness, and self-control' (Gal. 5:22–3).

Paul's use of metamorphosis, while it has no direct link to the transfiguration of Jesus, is firmly grounded in Christology. Christ is the image of God's glory (*eikôn*, see 4:4; 1 Cor. 11:7) and it is therefore Christ's face that believers behold as in a mirror (see 1 Cor. 13:12),[53] conforming them to his image: 'Christ is God's image because he is God's Son ... in whom God is beheld, and the image into which believers *are being transformed* is the *same* one they see mirrored there.'[54] Seeing is believing, in Paul's view.[55] To behold Christ as the representative of the new order is to move from the old age of which Adam is the representative (Rom. 5:12–21; 1 Cor. 15:21–2). Paul reiterates the role of the Spirit,[56] who is the source of the new age and its transfiguring freedom (3:18c).

In the last verse of the unit, Paul sums up his ministry in language that expresses, in almost lyrical terms, the content and goal of Christian proclamation (4:6). The symbolism of light and glory is a re-statement of Christ as the image of God (3:18; 4:4) and once more Paul draws on the figure of Moses, as well as the creation account in Genesis 1:3.[57] Jesus' face is unveiled because there is no need to hide the passing of the glory since it is abiding, definitive, eternal. What is remarkable here is the way the symbolism parallels the transfiguration story. The allusions to Moses on Mount Sinai, the imagery of the shining face, the glory of God physically manifest in Christ, the idea of metamorphosis, are all characteristic features of the transfiguration. The parallelism suggests that Paul, like John, knows something of the transfiguration tradition even if he does not quote it directly.[58]

The second passage is less immediately relevant for our purpose, because of the absence of most of the symbols associated with the transfiguration, except for the word 'transfigure'. Paul is nearing the end of his epistle to the Romans and moving from a theological discussion of the place of Israel (Rom. 10–11) to the implications of his theology of God's righteousness for Christian living (12:1–15:13):

> Therefore, I beseech you, brothers and sisters, through the mercies of God to present your bodies as a living sacrifice, holy, well-pleasing to God, your reasonable worship. 2 And do not be conformed to this age but be transfigured in newness of mind so that you may discern what is the will of God, that which is good, well-pleasing and perfect. (Rom. 12:1–2)

Once more, what lies behind Paul's encouragement of the Church is the contrast between life in the new age and life in the old. Paul speaks of Christian life as a form of worship in which 'Christians who strive to do what is right give a cultic sense to their lives' (Rom. 12:1).[59] This stands in contrast to the sacrifice of dead animals in temples, pagan or Jewish. Indeed, the whole of Christian living, Paul claims, is concerned with transfiguration: moving from the prison of the old order ('this world') to the freedom and love of the new. This is an inner transfiguration of heart, effected by the Spirit, not an outward one of mere appearance. Such transformation involves doing the will of God, the freedom of the new age making true obedience both desirable and possible. Thus Christians are no longer trapped, no longer powerless to do the will of God (Rom. 7:14–25), but are able to do 'what is good, well-pleasing and perfect' in God's sight (12:2). On this basis, Paul encourages them to live the life of the new age into which they have been baptized (see Rom. 6:1–11). The verb is in the imperative, 'be transfigured' (*metamorphousthe*, 12:2), implying a dedicated commitment to the Spirit's transforming power.

The path of metamorphosis is not merely – or even primarily – a matter of individual conversion, but concerns the salvation of the whole community as the body of Christ. In the following verses, Paul speaks of the gifts of Christ which are given for the good of the 'body' (12:4–8; see 1 Cor. 12:12–31). The greatest of these gifts and thus the strongest evidence of transfiguration is love (1 Cor. 13:1–13), a love that leads to compassion, harmony, humility, goodness, peace and justice, and eschews the path of arrogance, wrath and vengeance (12:14–21). Transformation does not mean the rejection of the law but rather its fulfilment in love (13:8–10), donning 'the armour of light' and forsaking the destructive life of 'the flesh' (13:11–14). A life of transfiguration is thus an ecclesial life. As part of the body, Christians are to become more and more like Christ, 'putting on the Lord Jesus Christ' (13:14) and exchanging the values of the world for God's righteousness as revealed in Christ and manifest in the life of the Spirit.[60] The second Pauline passage is important because, though more remotely connected to the transfiguration story, it makes clear that metamorphosis, grounded in Christology, is an essential characteristic of Christian living.

One further passage from the New Testament may be briefly mentioned. Here the language is markedly apocalyptic and the imagery consonant with the transfiguration story. The passage forms part of the opening vision of the Apocalypse or Book of Revelation, immediately preceding the letters to the seven Churches (Apoc. 2–3), and indeed part of their introduction:

> 12 And I turned to see the voice which was speaking to me, and having turned I saw seven golden lamp-stands 13 and in the midst of the lamp-stands was one like a Son of Man clothed in a long robe, with a golden belt around his breast. 14 His head and hair were white as white wool, as snow, and his eyes were like a flame of fire 15 and his feet like burnished bronze, burned in a furnace, and his voice was as the voice of many waters, 16 and he was holding in his right hand seven stars and from his mouth a sharp two-edged sword was coming forth and his face was as the sun shines in its power. 17 And when I saw him, I fell at his feet as one dead, and he placed his right hand upon me, saying, 'Do not fear; I am the First and the Last 18 and the Living One; and I was dead and behold I am alive for ages of ages, and I have the keys of death and of the Underworld. (Apoc. 1:12–18)

The symbolism of the passage has its origins in Jewish apocalyptic and particularly the Book of Daniel, with its the focus on the future coming of the Son of Man (1:7; Dan. 7:13). Yet the imagery is not so very different from the transfiguration. The appearance of Christ is more detailed in its description but is of the same kind: the whiteness and brightness of his head and face, which is compared to wool and snow, and the brilliance of the sun (1:14, 16b); the imagery of fire associated with his eyes and feet (1:14–15) which parallels that of light; his possession of the light of seven stars (1:16a), while standing in a circle of seven lamp-stands that represent the seven churches (1:12–13). The powerful light symbolism depicts the triumphant Christ who possesses sovereignty over life and death and is surrounded by representatives of the angelic host and the Church (1:20).

Are there indications here that the writer of the Apocalypse knew the transfiguration tradition? We have already seen the influence of apocalyptic imagery on the story of the transfiguration, imagery that suffuses the Apocalypse. Yet there is also an epiphanic quality to the passage. Jesus' true identity is revealed as 'the faithful witness, the firstborn from the dead, and the ruler of the kings of the earth' (1:5), who is closely associated with God as 'the Alpha and Omega … the All-ruling One' (1:8). Following the letter to the Churches is a further apocalyptic vision of Jesus as the Lamb who, because he alone is able to open the seven seals of the scroll (5:6–14), is worthy of the same worship as God (5:6b–11). The primary reference is to Christ's triumph over death in the resurrection, but there is also an anticipation of the parousia in the depiction of the one who is 'the First and the Last' (1:17). The eschatology is Christological, grounded in Jesus' intimate relationship to God which makes him the co-equal recipient of the Church's worship. Epiphany and apocalyptic vision here go hand-in-hand.

The passage displays a series of images that are parallel to the transfiguration. This could well be explained by the fact that John the Seer is drawing on the same traditions, including the paschal mystery. Yet the resurrection accounts in the Gospels do not explicitly depict Jesus in white clothing or with radiant features; such description is reserved for the transfiguration. Perhaps, indeed, it is the glorious Jesus of the transfiguration that enables the New Testament writers to associate him with the glory of the parousia. If such were the case, the imagery of the transfiguration – if not its actual narrative – is known as much to John the Seer as to the Gospel writers, including the closely related Gospel of John. This is admittedly speculative, but it does locate the source of such imagery in the life and ministry of Jesus, rather than extrapolating it from the resurrection. It is more likely that the parousia is a conscious, theological projection of the transfiguration, via the resurrection, than that the resurrection has been projected back onto Jesus' life and ministry.

The Christological imagery of the Apocalypse, moreover, is profoundly ecclesial. The apocalyptic vision of Jesus is revealed in the context of the letters to Christian communities in Asia Minor, struggling against the idolatry and oppression of the Roman empire. The vision is given to John of

Patmos, suffering for his faithfulness to Christ (1:9–11). As with the three disciples in Matthew's account, after the vision of Jesus' glory, John the Seer falls at his feet, overcome by fear, and is raised and comforted by the approach of the Lord (1:17; Matt. 17:7). The word of consolation – like the words of challenge in the ensuing letters to the churches – comes from the One in whose mouth is a two-edged sword (1:16; see Heb. 4:12–13), whose salvation both judges and gives life, enabling the Church to stand firm against all that threatens it, from within and without. Although (once more) explicit language of transfiguration is absent, the idea of deepening fidelity to the gospel is not, representing parallel notions of transformation and change. The glorious revelation of Christ is the glorification also of the Church (1:5–6), as it is of the disciples on the mount of transfiguration.

Alongside the Gospel of John, these (and other) passages give valuable insight into the meaning of transfiguration, suggesting a widespread awareness of the story in the early Church. The Fourth Gospel uses the symbolism of revelation and glory across the entire narrative of the Gospel, showing that the identity and destiny of Jesus are not restricted to one incident but luminously present in the incarnation itself. The two Pauline references are very different from the transfiguration in the Gospels in many respects, yet their concern with discipleship and the life of the Church shows that transfiguration symbolism applies to believers as well as Christ, and that Christian transformation is the goal of God's revelation in Christ. The opening vision of the Apocalypse confirms the same Christological imagery, with its emphasis on the glorious triumph of Jesus' life and death, and the eschatological implications for struggling Christian communities. Indeed, theologically – as we will see in the next chapter – the one is dependent on the other. Christology lies at the heart of the transfiguration in the New Testament, a Christology linked, on the one side, to God and the Spirit and, on the other side, to the transformation of believers.

Notes

1 Smith, D. M., *Johannine Christianity: Essays on Its Setting, Sources, and Theology*, T. & T. Clark, Edinburgh, 1984, 95–172. Barrett, C. K., *The Gospel According to St. John: An Introduction with Commentary and Notes on the Greek Text*, 2nd edn, SPCK, London, 1978, 42–54, is unusual in arguing for John's dependence on Mark.

2 The view is strengthened if Luke too is dependent on more than one tradition.

3 Further on this, see Lee, D., 'Transfiguration and the Gospel of John', in Kendall, D. and O'Collins, G. (eds), *In Many and Diverse Ways: A Festschrift Honoring Jacques Dupuis*, Orbis, Maryknoll, NY, 2003, 158–69.

4 See Kooy, V. H., 'The Transfiguration Motif in the Gospel of John', in Cook, J. I. (ed.), *Saved by Hope*, Eerdmans, Grand Rapids, MI, 1978, 64–78; also Caird, G. B., 'The Transfiguration', *Expository Times* 67, 1955–6, 294 and Barrett, *St John*, 53.

5 Ramsay, M., *The Glory of God and the Transfiguration of Christ*, 2nd edn, Darton, Longman & Todd, London, 1967, 123.

6 As we have seen, not all these elements are present in the narrative of 2 Peter.

7 For Kooy, *op. cit.*, 64–78, the transfiguration underlies five passages: Prologue (1:1–14), Cana (2:11), Lazarus (11:4, 40), coming of the Greeks (12:20–47), and farewell discourse (13:1–17:26).

8 Schnelle, U., *Das Evangelium nach Johannes*, Evangelische Verlagsanstalt, Leipzig, 1998, 29.

9 Schmidt, T. E., 'The Penetration of Barriers and the Revelation of Christ in the Gospels', *Novum Testamentum* 34, 1992, 245.

10 There is no 'but' at John 1:17 between Moses and Jesus, who are on the same side (5:45–7). For Moses, A. D. A., *Matthew's Transfiguration Story and Jewish–Christian Controversy* (ed. S. E. Porter), Sheffield Academic Press, Sheffield, 1996, 217–19, there are Sinai motifs lying behind John 1:14 (cf. Exod. 3:6–7).

11 Bultmann, R. *The Gospel of John* (trans. G. R. Beasley-Murray), Blackwell, Oxford, 1971, 60–1.

12 The eleventh-century Ottonian manuscript shows the nativity above the transfiguration with the words of John 1:14; Nes, S., *The Uncreated Light: An Iconographical Study of the Transfiguration in the Eastern Church*, Eastern Christian Publications, Fairfax, VA, 2002, 19–23, 29–38. See Origen, *Against Celsus* 6.68, in McGuckin, J. A., *The Transfiguration of Christ in Scripture and Tradition*, Edwin Mellen, Lewiston, NY, 1986, 154.

13 No more than John, however, does Paul divorce soul and body (Rom. 7:14–8:17, 1 Cor. 3:2–3, Gal. 5:16–26).

14 See Kooy, *op. cit.*, 67–9.

15 For a survey of 'flesh' throughout John's Gospel, see Lee, D., *Flesh and Glory: Symbol, Gender and Theology in the Gospel of John*, Crossroad, New York, 2002, 29–64.

16 See John 1:14; 2:11; 5:41, 44; 7:18; 8:50, 54; 9:24; 11:4, 40; 12:41; 43; 17:5, 22, 24.

17 See John 7:39; 8:54; 11:4; 12:16, 23, 28; 13:31; 32; 14:13; 15:8; 16:14; 17:1, 4, 5, 10; 21:19.

18 Schnelle, U., *Antidocetic Christology in the Gospel of John: An Investigation of the Place of the Fourth Gospel in the Johannine School* (trans. L. M. Maloney), Fortress, Minneapolis, MN, 1992, 81.

19 Kooy, op. cit., 76, and Moses, *op. cit.*, 220–1.

20 Gregory of Nazianzus, 'On the Holy Passover Xl v.633–636', in Migne, J.-P. (ed.), *Patrologia Graeca*, 36.

21 Schneiders, S. M., *Written That You May Believe: Encountering Jesus in the Fourth Gospel*, Crossroad, New York, 1999, 74.

22 Moloney, F. J., *The Gospel of John*, Liturgical Press, Collegeville, MN, 1998, 68.

23 See Moloney, F. J., *Signs and Shadows: Reading John 5–12*, Fortress, Minneapolis, MN, 1996, 152–3.

24 On the symbolic and narrative dimensions of John 6, see Lee, D., *The Symbolic Narratives of the Fourth Gospel: The Interplay of Form and Meaning*, Sheffield Academic Press, Sheffield, 1994, 126–60.

25 Unlike the Synoptic accounts which locate the feedings in the wilderness (see Mark 6:32; 8:4).

26 The Wisdom/Sophia overtones are strong here; see Scott, M., *Sophia and the Johannine Jesus*, Sheffield Academic Press, Sheffield, 1992, 116–19. On the suggestions of breastfeeding in the eucharistic language, see Ford, J. M., *Redeemer, Friend and Mother: Salvation in Antiquity and in John*, Fortress, Minneapolis, MN, 1997, 127–31.

27 See Thompson, M.M., *The God of the Gospel of John*, Eerdmans, Grand Rapids, MI, 2001, 78–9: 'the unity of the life-giving *work* of Father and Son ... also predicates a remarkable status of the Son, one which is not made of any other creature. The Son "has life in himself".'

28 Moloney, *John*, 351–3.

29 On transfiguration elements here, see Bultmann, *The Gospel of John*, 428, and Brown, R. E., *The Gospel According to John*, 2 vols, Doubleday, New York, 1966, vol. 1, 476. The link is apparent in the Lukan disciples' somnolence (Luke 9:32).

30 'All things' may well be the original reading; so Beasley-Murray, G. R., *John*, Word Books, Waco, TX, 1987, 205.

31 At Tabernacles, water was taken each morning from Siloam and poured over the altar; each evening the temple was flooded with light;

see Yee, G. A., *Jewish Feasts and the Gospel of John*, Michael Glazier, Wilmington, DE, 1989, 70–82.

32 See Kooy, *op. cit.*, 69–70.

33 So Brouwer, W., *The Literary Development of John 13–17: A Chiastic Reading*, Society of Biblical Literature, Atlanta, GA, 2000, 9–10, 117–18; also Moloney, *John*, 477–9.

34 For Schnackenburg, R., *The Gospel According to St. John*, 3 vols, Burns & Oates, London, 1968–82, vol. 3, 167–202, it is 'the prayer of the departing Redeemer', since 'high priestly prayer' is not Johannine. For parallels with the Lord's Prayer, see Perkins, P., 'The Gospel According to John', in Brown, R. E. et al. (eds), *The New Jerome Biblical Commentary*, Geoffrey Chapman, London, 1990, 978.

35 See Dodd, C. H., *The Interpretation of the Fourth Gospel*, Cambridge University Press, Cambridge, 1953, 419–20.

36 On this translation of *pros* (meaning, 'towards'), see de la Potterie, I., 'L'emploi de *eis* dans Saint Jean et ses incidences théologiques', *Biblica* 43, 1962, 366–87.

37 For the minority view that 'all flesh' includes all created beings, see Whitacre, R. A., *John*, InterVarsity Fellowship, Leicester, 1999, 404, and Lee, *Flesh and Glory*, 43–5.

38 The arresting party is so overcome by Jesus' 'I am' that they fall down (18:4–8).

39 Yet at the cross Jesus is not abandoned either by the Father or his disciples (16:32; 19:25–30).

40 On these symbols, see Brown, R.E., *The Death of the Messiah – From Gethsemane to the Grave: A Commentary on the Passion Narratives in the Four Gospels*, 2 vols, Doubleday, New York, 1994, vol. 2, 955–8, 1019–26, 1069–78, 1082–3, 1178–82

41 Schnelle, *Antidocetic Christology*, 209.

42 See Ashton, J., *Understanding the Fourth Gospel*, Clarendon, Oxford, 1990, 383–406.

43 Schnackenburg, vol. 2, 437.

44 Thomas's confession of faith brings the Gospel back to its beginning (1:1–2, 18).

45 See Nes, *op. cit.*, 53.

46 For a summary of the problems of the passage, see Wright, N. T., 'Reflected Glory: 2 Cor. 3:18' in Hurst, L. D. and Wright, N. T. (eds), *The Glory of Christ in the New Testament: Studies in Christology in Memory of George Bradford Caird*, Clarendon, Oxford, 1987, 141–2.

47 Furnish, P. V., *II Corinthians: A New Translation with Introduction and Commentary*, Doubleday, New York, 1984, 232.

48 Paul may have invented the phrase 'old covenant' for the law; see Murphy-O'Connor, J., 'The Second Letter to the Corinthians', in Brown, R. E. et al. (eds), *The New Jerome Biblical Commentary*, Geoffrey Chapman, London, 1990, 820.

49 'The Lord' probably refers to God; Furnish, *op. cit.*, 211–12, 234–5, and Murphy-O'Connor, 'The Second Letter to the Corinthians', 820.

50 Note the contrast between the fading glory of Moses and the glory of God in Christ which not only abides but increases; so Furnish, *op. cit.*, 215, and Plummer, A. et al. (eds), *A Critical and Exegetical Commentary on the Second Epistle of St. Paul to the Corinthians*, T. & T. Clark, Edinburgh, 1915, 107.

51 E.g. 'conformed' (*symmorphos*, Rom. 8:29; Phil. 3:21), 'to be conformed' (*symmorphizesthai*, Phil. 3:10), 'to form' (*morphoun*, Gal. 4:19), 'to change' (*allassein*, 1 Cor. 15:51–2).

52 Cyril of Alexandria, *Diverse Homilies* 9, and Jerome, *Commentary on 2 Corinthians c.3* and *Commentary on Philippians c.3*, in McGuckin, *op. cit.*, 179, 273–4.

53 Wright, 'Reflected Glory', 144–5, suggests that the image and the mirror refer to Christians, who perceive the face of Christ in one another.

54 Furnish, *op. cit.*, 215.

55 The Hellenistic view was that to see the gods was transformative; so also Judaism (1 Enoch 28:4; 51:45; 108:13; 2 Apoc. Bar. 51:3, 10); *ibid.*, 240–1.

56 The meaning of the final phrase is difficult; see Plummer et al., *Second Corinthians*, 108–9.

57 Barrett, C. K., *A Commentary on the Second Epistle to the Corinthians*, A. & C. Black, London, 1973, 134–5.

58 So Wenham, D. and Moses, A. D. A., '"There Are Some Standing Here …": Did They Become the "Reputed Pillars" of the Jerusalem Church? Some Reflections on Mark 9:1, Galatians 2:9 and the Transfiguration', *Novum Testamentum* 36, 1994, 163. Paul makes few allusions to Jesus' ministry. It is possible that this language reflects Paul's own conversion (Acts 9:1–9; cf. 22:6–16; 26:12–18); see Moses, *op. cit.*, 244.

59 Fitzmyer, J. A., 'The Letter to the Romans', in Brown, R. E. et al. (eds), *The New Jerome Biblical Commentary*, Geoffrey Chapman, London, 1990, 862.

60 Ramsay, *op. cit.*, 126–7, cites Hebrews 2:5–9 as a possible parallel to the transfiguration. The language, however, seems to point to the ascension. A more likely parallel is 1 John 3:2.

6
The Transfiguration in Symbol and Theology

The transfiguration occupies a central place in biblical theology. Its pivotal location in the Synoptic Gospels and 2 Peter, its clarity in the texture of the Fourth Gospel, and hints of its symbolic presence elsewhere in the New Testament, encourage us to draw the story from the dim and dusty wings onto centre stage. In this final chapter, therefore, it is necessary to gather together the various threads of the transfiguration and weave a fabric that will accommodate its intricate lines and colours. By itself, the exploration of a biblical motif such as the transfiguration across a number of texts is meagre and deficient without the attempt to understand its coherence and contribution to theology and worship. The neglect of the transfiguration, at least in the West, makes this task even more imperative. The transfiguration story, with its wealth of symbolism, has something vital to say about divine glory and human transformation, about the body and the earth, and about the beauty and light that have their origins in God alone.

There are more ways than one of interpreting the transfiguration, both in the four explicit narratives we have examined and in the use of the tradition elsewhere in the New Testament. However, the transfiguration allows for more than one idea to be entertained: symbols are not easily restricted to one meaning.[1] We have already seen that the transfiguration crosses two literary genres: epiphany and apocalyptic vision. These two symbolic approaches need not be regarded as mutually exclusive but can be viewed as complementary. Furthermore, the transfiguration story also addresses the fear and frailty of the disciples, adding an ecclesial or anthropological dimension, with ecological implications. This makes three ways of reading the transfiguration: (1) the apocalyptic, which concerns theology proper (the revelation of God's own self); (2) the epiphanic, which deals with Christology and the revelation of Jesus' identity; and (3) the anthropological, with its emphasis on the restoration of 'all flesh'. Together they form a rich tapestry of meaning and allusion.

The first aspect of the transfiguration is its use of apocalyptic symbolism. Images of light and glory, shining clothes and face, transformation and revelation, all point to God's future reign. The vision on the mountain is eschatological, depicting the radiance of the end time and the final coming of Christ. At the same time, it points to the resurrection in which God triumphs over sin, death and suffering, and to the ascension where humanity is caught up into the very being of God. In this sense, Jesus' transfiguration is rather like looking into a crystal ball – except that what is foretold is not the future of our making but God's. In the transfiguration, we turn our gaze towards a future in which God's kingdom will finally dawn, bringing to an end the reign of evil and suffering, and replacing it with God's sovereign dominion of righteousness, peace, and salvation. The transfiguration is the promise of what is to come.

Yet the apocalyptic symbolism does more than direct our gaze to the future. The final coming of God's reign is linked inextricably to the presence of Jesus on the mountain. As we saw with 2 Peter, the transfiguration is not just a sneak preview. It enters definitely into the present from its home in the future, but the transformation it points to is already shaping the world, already anticipating that divine future. The transfiguration, in this sense, functions as a religious symbol which points to and yet bears within it a transcendent reality,[2] making God's future vibrantly present. The reader is shaped by the symbols – turned, as it were, to face the right direction, that of Christ's re-appearing. Just as our own past shapes our present identity, so too does God's future. In Christ, the new age has already begun and the Church lives in the interface between a future that has come into being and a future that is still to be. By entering into the experience of the disciples on the mountain, the reader enters the realm of God's future in Christ.

The apocalyptic aspects of the symbolism, however, are not primarily Christological. Apocalyptic is fundamentally *theological* in its orientation – that is to say, it focuses on God and God's ultimate triumph. Perhaps, in Mark and Matthew's accounts of the transfiguration, we need to give the verb 'and was transfigured' its full force (Mark 9:2; Matt. 17:2). As a 'divine passive', the verb speaks of God's action on Jesus, God's revelation of the future in Jesus' metamorphosis. The light and glory of the transfiguration are not decorative elements added to a message that is to be located elsewhere, but rather core symbols. They point to a future where God's salvation will triumph definitively over evil and suffering, where God's glory will suffuse all things and all people – in Paul's language (in another apocalyptic context), a future where God will be 'all in all' (1 Cor. 15:28).

What this means is that the transfiguration, within its apocalyptic framework, conveys a profound message of hope. For all their misunderstanding, incoherence, confusion and fear, the three disciples on the mountain are given a vision of hope and joyful expectation. It is indeed 'good' for them to be present at such a vision of the future, because it gives them the basis for their own proclamation of the good news. The transfiguration may overwhelm and even dismay them, but it also offers them hope. These same disciples will lose sight of that hope in the horror of the passion,[3] but it will come to meet them again in the resurrection, offering a joyful outlook on the future, despite the inevitability of suffering and persecution. The palpable hope of the transfiguration will rise up after Easter to sustain and enliven them, as part of the core of their faith. The apocalyptic symbols of the transfiguration thus communicate the triumph of God's future, enacted in Christ, even as he embarks on the path of suffering and death. They are a potent reminder that God's last word in Christ is one of life and joy, whatever else may intervene.

There is a further dimension to the apocalyptic symbolism, which is part of its re-shaping under the influence of Christian theology. The vision on the mountain is complicated by the concurrent interplay of past and future, the old age and the new age, which in Christ converge. It is also complicated by the reality of the cross which combines with the apocalyptic elements to ensure 'the unity of the Cross and the parousia'.[4] In the Synoptic Gospels, the transfiguration marks the beginning of Jesus' journey to Jerusalem, a theme made clear in the narrative context of Mark and Matthew, but even more explicit in Luke's version from the subject of conversation between Jesus, Moses and Elijah (Luke 9:31), where Jesus' departure – its manner and meaning – provides an interpretative key. The 'labour pains' that Mark speaks of later in his Gospel, the suffering that signals and indeed brings to birth the end time (Mark 13:8), refer first and foremost to the suffering of Jesus on the cross, the turning point of the ages. Jesus descends into the sin and suffering of the old age (as symbolized in his baptism), defeating it from within, and rises into the new age which he inaugurates. The one who ascends to the heights also descends to the depths. The suffering that is to be expected in apocalyptic literature is hereby focused on Jesus' own suffering, which is redemptive and liberating. In the Gospels, there is no glory without the cross, and no cross without glory. The one who is transfigured on the mountain is the one who is disfigured by anguish, pain and death on the cross. The two cannot be separated.

Jesus climbs to the heights, therefore, before he descends to the depths, the one as necessary as the other in the Synoptic accounts. Only in the context of God's ultimate triumph can Jesus walk the way of the cross, in obedience to the Father's will, waging the final battle against evil, taking on the demons and the anguish of suffering and despair. The glory of the mountain is the glory he will receive on the other side of death, and also at the world's end. The light that shines from his face and clothing shines because he is first prepared to face the darkness, illuminating it with the triumphant light and love of God. In this sense, the glory we see on the mountain is the anticipated glory of the crucified Lord, risen and ascended, possessing sovereignty over the living and the dead (Apoc. 1:12–18).

The second aspect of the transfiguration derives from its character as an epiphany. Through its symbols, the story discloses the identity of Jesus on the mountain, an identity manifest in every detail. This dimension is the main perspective of the earliest Christian interpreters of the transfiguration.[5] It is also a prominent part of contemporary Eastern Orthodox interpretation in which the transfiguration is central. Indeed, from early days, the transfiguration in the East 'came to be treated less as an event amongst other events and a dogma amongst other dogmas than a symbol of something which pervades all dogma and all worship'.[6] The change in Jesus' bodily appearance, extending to his clothing and also (in Matthew and Luke) his face, is itself a complex symbol. In addition to the apocalyptic indications of the radiant garments of the righteous at the end time, the intense whiteness of Jesus' body indicates that his identity is to be framed, not only in terms of his human existence, but also in relation to the divine world. Jesus belongs elsewhere as much as he belongs here. Indeed, his stance on the mountain, on the boundary between heaven and earth, confirms that his home is to be found on both sides of the gulf. The other symbols make the same point. The presence of the two greatest prophets of Israel's past, Moses and Elijah, acting as Jesus' attendants and (according to Luke) discussing his 'exodus' in Jerusalem, reveals his communion with the celestial world, a world in which time and space have no boundaries. The overshadowing cloud, which is miraculous in all three Synoptic accounts and, in Matthew's version, paradoxically shares the same brightness as Jesus' appearance, is symbolic of the heavenly realm and its nearness to Jesus. And finally the voice from the cloud (or, as in 2 Peter, from heaven) corroborates the Christological meaning of the other symbols, this time specifying that Jesus is not simply one heavenly being among others but the divine Son, whose communion with the Father gives him a sublime identity that transcends any other.

From this perspective, the mountain symbolism does not bestow a new identity on Jesus, as the parallels to the baptism and (in Matthew and Luke) the birth narratives make clear. Rather, the transfiguration reveals Jesus' full identity – as if the air on the mountain were clearer for the onlooker and the perception keener. John's Gospel, with its analogous symbolism, emphasizes the same dimension of the transformation. Jesus' flesh is the place where the divine glory abides, a glory associated with the tabernacle in the wilderness and the temple on Mount Sion, the mountain of God, the locus of God's dwelling in Israel. Indeed, the central symbol of the Fourth Gospel is that the divine Word has crossed the divide between divine and human and entered the domain of matter. In the incarnation, the glory of God gleams through the flesh of Jesus; in symbolic and metaphorical terms, the flesh becomes the medium of divine glory.[7] The single moment of epiphany on the mount of transfiguration in the Synoptic Gospels is the place where the disciples receive the true perception of Jesus' divinely human glory, enabling them to interpret the whole of his life and death in that light, as well as in the light of God's luminous future. In John's Gospel, the glory of God is fully manifest in the person of Jesus, equally dazzling in all he says and does throughout his ministry, and resplendent in his death on the cross. In this Gospel, from beginning to end, Jesus is the Light of the world (8:12; 9:5). John gazes at Jesus not just as the human being whose flesh, in a sense, is 'transfigured' to proclaim divine glory (to the believing eye) but also as the Word whose being is changed to take on mortal flesh. Although John does not use explicit language of transfiguration in relation to Jesus, as we have observed, he stresses both aspects in his use of glory, a glory he sees as radically present in the incarnation.[8] In Paul's language – under the influence of the transfiguration tradition – Jesus is revealed as the true 'image' of God, the one whose shining face reflects the unfading glory of God, partially but never fully or permanently divulged in Moses (2 Cor. 3:18; 4:4).

In this context, the New Testament symbol of sonship, associated with all four transfiguration accounts, needs to be given its due weight. The title is supported by the adjective 'beloved' (or 'chosen', as in Luke 9:35), becoming virtually a title in its own right in 2 Peter. Sharing a distinct relationship to God, Jesus is revealed to the disciples as the chosen, beloved Son. In line with the baptism, the title refers not only to Jesus' central role in the reign or kingdom of God but also to an identity that is unique, beyond that of Moses or Elijah. While at one level, Jesus as Son is representative of Israel (especially in Matthew and Luke), there is a deeper sense in which that sonship spans the two realms of earth and heaven. Although more explicit than the Synoptics, John's Gospel shares the same view of the uniqueness of Jesus as the divine Son. From this angle, the transfiguration may be termed a 'theophany', the unmistakable revelation of the Father through the divinely human person of the Son, who is the definitive symbol of God. This interpretation of the transfiguration is present from the earliest days in both East and West, including in the Protestant Reformers (Luther, Thomas Müntzer).[9]

The epiphanic dimension to the transfiguration, moreover, has as its centre the symbol of light. As Mark's Gospel makes plain in its image of the bleacher, the light of the transfiguration is not conceived as a natural source of light. There is no natural (or, for that matter, historical) cause that can explain the symbols on the mountain, least of all the radiance of the light. Eastern theology speaks of this as the 'uncreated light' of God, a part of God's very self.[10] The light is neither material nor spiritual, because it transcends entirely the order of creation.[11] Nor can it be apprehended by the intellect alone:

> This light (*johôs*) ... can be defined as the visible quality of the divinity, of the energies or grace in which God makes Himself known. It is not a reality of the intellectual order ... Nor is it a reality of the sensible order. This light is a light which fills at the same time both intellect and senses, revealing itself to the whole man, and not only to one of his faculties. The divine light, being given in mystical experience, surpasses at the same time both sense and intellect. It is immaterial and is not apprehended by the senses.[12]

Yet the divine light is also eschatological, an epiphany of God's glorious future, depicting 'the beauty of the Age to Come' when 'the most holy Transfiguration will continually and endlessly dazzle us'.[13] So the light of the holy mountain shines from the eternal realm, an epiphany that defines the shape and form of God's eschatological reign: 'the first epiphany, as yet hidden ... kindles in the believers the active love which is also a yearning for the second epiphany'.[14]

Those present at the transfiguration, at least in the Gospel accounts, are overwhelmed by what they see and hear, by the light and by the voice.

Yet it is not only the intensity of the radiance that renders them prostrate. It is also the beauty of Christ on the mountain-top, a beauty associated with light and glory, and confirmed in the speech of the divine voice: 'that inconceivable beauty, the highest and most precious of all things that are desirable, which brings ceaseless joy to all who look upon it'.[15] This aspect of the transfiguration has not always been taken seriously, especially in those traditions which regard beauty with suspicion.[16] Yet its presence seems inescapable (even if implicit) in the Synoptic narrative, encapsulating both the Christological and anthropological dimensions of the transfiguration.

There are, in general terms, two aspects to beauty in a theological understanding. In the first place, beauty consists of the union of form (*species*) and splendour (*lumen*),[17] the outer contours and inner content, the external structure and interior light. The presence of such beauty at the transfiguration is palpable in the body of Jesus as it becomes translucent, redolent with light, depicting most winsomely the union of divine and human, glory and flesh. From this perspective, the transfiguration becomes the epitome of incarnate beauty, the central symbol of form and splendour, uniting heaven and earth. At the same time, the beauty of the transfiguration is not decorative or incidental, but rather substantial, grounded in the being of God, an aspect of divine glory.[18] Indeed, the close association between the glory on the mountain and the suffering of the cross indicates that this divine beauty – unlike secular understandings – embraces 'death as well as life, fear as well as joy, what we might call the ugly as well as what we might call the beautiful'.[19] In this embrace of love, form itself (*morphê*) is trans-formed (*metamorphousthai*).[20]

Second, beauty gives rise to a subjective experience of rapture, the sense of being transported beyond the boundaries of the self.[21] There is no neutral or disinterested stance here. The rapture is linked to absolute love (*eros/amor*) which is itself the ground of both creation and incarnation:

> we must dare to affirm ... that the Creator of the Universe himself, in his beautiful and good Eros towards the Universe, is, through his excessive erotic Goodness, transported outside of himself, in his providential activities towards all things that have being, and is overcome by the sweet spell of Goodness, Love, and Eros. In this manner, he is drawn from his transcendent throne above all things to dwell within the heart of all things.[22]

The rapture that draws God, as it were, out of heaven to earth also draws the believer out of an enclosed selfhood into the beauty and luminosity of God. Towards this rapture – the beauty of the life of God – Jesus leads his faltering disciples, as he ascends the mount of transfiguration. Here beauty is closely linked, not only to love and yearning, but also to pleasure, enjoyment and ecstasy, an experience that is as much sensuous as spirited. A theological understanding of beauty, profoundly relevant to the transfiguration, thus signifies

> [a] 'coming to see' the form in which God's Word comes to us, gives itself to us and loves us. In this act of seeing, there already lies the 'rapture': a breaking out from ourselves in the power of our being called and affected, in the power of the divine love which draws near to us and enables us to receive itself.[23]

There is clearly a profound sense of beauty in the transfiguration, a beauty that has its source and provenance in God's own self. That beauty includes its desirability, the physical form that inhabits yet transcends the sensory world, and its goodness, which is inseparable from truth.[24] The adjective *kalos* in Greek, as we have already seen, originally meant 'beautiful' as well as 'good'. Peter's exclamation, 'It is good for us to be here' (Mark 9:5) conveys a sense of the beauty of the transfiguration as well as its inherent goodness. What the transfiguration reveals is the beauty of God in the mystery of the incarnation, the splendour of divine glory and uncreated light – the beauty and glory, in other words, of revelation itself.[25] But it is also the beauty of a humanity and a creation restored in Christ: 'the original beauty of the image'.[26] The beauty of the image, lost in the fall, is restored to the cosmos by the one who is himself the Image of God, transfigured in radiant splendour on the mountain.

The third dimension of the transfiguration – which we have already begun to touch upon – is its anthropology. The symbols of the transfiguration open the door to the transformation of human beings as a consequence of Jesus' own metamorphosis, the former dependent entirely on the latter. The symbolic structure of the transfiguration presupposes the fallenness of the world and the alienation of human beings from God. All the New Testament accounts of the transfiguration assume this point. The three on the mountain in the Synoptics are representative disciples and apostles; their awareness, via Peter, of the goodness of the event is offset by their misunderstanding, indicating their own need of transformation.

Matthew emphasizes this ecclesial dimension, with the close link to Jesus' founding of the Church in the preceding episode (Matt. 16:18–19), asserting its authority over the threatening powers of the Underworld. For 2 Peter, the apostolic testimony to the parousia signifies that which shapes Christian living into God's future as against those in the community who would deny such hope. For Mark, the misunderstanding of the disciples is most painfully apparent, requiring nothing less than the transforming presence of the risen Christ in Galilee (Mark 14:28; 16:7). For Luke, Jesus and the disciples descend the mountain following the transfiguration to find a situation of desperation – a demon-possessed child whom even the disciples cannot relieve; their journey to Jerusalem will lead Jesus into the lions' den.

What this means is that the symbols of the transfiguration address the world precisely at the point of its disfiguration. This disfiguration, already indicated in the disciples' misunderstanding, is vividly apparent in the Synoptic placing of the transfiguration at the beginning of the journey to Jerusalem, where Jesus will be handed over to sinners. The cross is the revelation equally of divine love and of the tragedy of sin and suffering in the world. Christians are summoned out of this tragedy to live the life of God. Eastern Orthodoxy refers to this dimension as 'deification', following the language of 2 Peter where Christians are called to become 'sharers in the divine nature' (2 Pet. 1:4); in the West, the language is that of sanctification and holiness. Peter, James and John represent the Church and therefore the breadth of humanity in its vocation to stand before the divine light that gleams from Jesus' body.

From a female point of view, this symbolic language may be deemed problematical. It would be easy to dismiss the transfiguration and its anthropology on the grounds that it depicts, in a representative capacity, only male persons: Jesus signifies God, Moses and Elijah stand for the people of Israel, Peter, James and John for the Church. The body that is metamorphosed and that emits radiant light is a male body. Against this, it could be argued that women are included in the representation, as full members of the people of God. But this argument, though not invalid (since representation is, by definition, restrictive), is insufficient in an anthropology that confirms the co-equal capacity of women and men to represent God, since both are made in the image of God (Gen. 1:26–7) and, through baptism, re-made in the image of Christ (Gal. 3:27–8). More pertinently, there are other narratives in the

Gospels that present women in such a representative role in, for example, the birth stories and the passion and resurrection narratives (e.g.
Luke 1:26–56; Mark 14:3–9; 15:40–1; 15:47–16:8). And it is true that
John, who omits the telling of the transfiguration story and uses the
imagery throughout his Gospel, is the most sympathetic to women's discipleship and ministry of all the Gospels. In a sense, we are left with the
problem, in the knowledge that the disfiguration of creation includes
the alienation and marginalization of women, even in stories that stand
at the heart of faith. Yet at its deepest level, the transfiguration has a
theological import that, while not rendering them irrelevant, ultimately transcends questions of ideology. The symbols of the transfiguration
have as much relevance for women, who possess the same capacity as
men to represent the people of God, both in their inadequacies and their
grace, and whose bodies are likewise destined for metamorphosis,
divinization and light.[27]

It is a terrible yet eloquent coincidence that the Feast of the
Transfiguration is universally celebrated on 6 August, Hiroshima Day,[28] a
day that stands as an emblem of the impersonal brutality of modern war-
fare. It is difficult for Christians to celebrate the transfiguration without
images of the gruesome disfiguring of human beings in the devastation of
war. The light of God, reflected in the face of Christ who is the source of
creation in its original goodness, turns its beams upon human beings at
the point of their violence and degradation, their oppression and escapism,
their loss and alienation, their fear, pride, anger and despair. The cross
embodies symbolically both dimensions, exhibiting human fear and violence as well as the divine will for salvation. In the end, human beings are
saved through the dual revelation of their own disfiguration and the hope
of their transfiguration in Christ. The poem 'August 6th' captures this
profound yet terrible dynamic:

> You put an Ohio Blue Tipped match
> To the black wick, and they are bonded in
> A momentary fireball, each the catch
> Of the other's fervour. Time now to begin
>
> The daily ritual, bread and wine on the table,
> A tale to be told of murder and its work
> Which, stultified and annulled, the spirit's Babel,
> Is overturned by the life it could not burke.

And you think, as on each such date, both of the one
Soon to go to the gallows-route, but shining
Briefly to hearten the few who had begun
To catch his version of love's contagion – of him,
And of the flash-kept moment still refining
A sea of fire not even the damned could swim.[29]

Both transfiguration and disfiguration are imaged here in symbols of fire and blazing light; yet whereas the one mutilates and destroys, the other (equally terrifying, though in a very different way) gives life at the very point of devastation.

The anthropological dimension of the transfiguration gives rise to the question of *how* the transfiguration and its symbolism can address the context of human disfiguration. The first answer, an apocalyptic one, is that the transfiguration holds out the promise of God's eschatological victory over death, and indeed over all that is destructive and life-denying in the old age. The transfiguration points forward symbolically to the empty tomb and Jesus' resurrection, and beyond that to the parousia. We have already seen that this gives the transfiguration an anticipatory function, a point that becomes clear immediately following Mark's account, where the disciples puzzle over Jesus' reference to his rising from the dead (Mark 9:9–10). Jesus transfigured on the mountain is the promise of God's salvation in which the disciples already participate. The mountain is thus the symbolic place of revelation, promising and anticipating a future world without suffering or violence, a place redolent with reconciliation, harmony, beauty and joy (see Isa. 2:2–4; 11:6–9; 25:6–10a). The very air is eschatological and the disciples breathe the atmosphere of God's renewed world. Their mere presence, however inadequate their response, engages the hope of their own transfiguration. This experience of being embraced by the celestial light of Christ is essentially transformative, like alchemists producing gold from base metal. As in a fairy tale, the mountain is a numinous place which points to the unexpectedly happy ending of the human story, the 'eucatastrophe' or good catastrophe of the gospel, where the misery and violence of the world are turned on their head and replaced by 'a piercing glimpse of joy, and heart's desire' that has its origins in God.[30]

The second answer to the how of the transfiguration is closer to the epiphanic and relates fundamentally to the incarnation. The Fourth Gospel's use of the symbolism makes this dimension plain: 'the Incarnation is a theological prerequisite for the Transfiguration.'[31] This

dimension is expressed in the theophany symbolism. As readers we do not
– indeed cannot – lose sight of the fact that, in distinction to the epiphany
of Abraham's mysterious three visitors (Gen. 18), the divine glory in the
transfiguration of Jesus is manifest in the flesh. The Synoptic motif of the
radiance of Jesus' clothing acts as a metonymy for Jesus' whole person, a
point more explicit in Matthew and Luke with the reference to Jesus'
transfigured face (Matt. 17:2; Luke 9:29). The metamorphosis of Jesus'
body makes of his physical reality the symbol through which the divine
splendour shines. Thus, his physicality – which is quintessential to any
definition of what it means to be human – becomes the icon of his celes-
tiality. The materiality of his appearance is a vital part of what the disciples see.[32] His body does not dissolve or become unreal; it bears within it
the wholeness of his humanity. Jesus' bodily identity is not presented on
the mountain peak as unreal or illusory; rather, his humanity remains
tangible, even while another identity illuminates it, the source of which
is God's own self. Jesus remains on earth, while standing on the threshold
of heaven.

The transfigured Jesus on the mountain, therefore, acts as the bridge
between heaven and earth. He is as conversant with the heavenly world as
with the earthly, able to speak concurrently with both the living and the
dead. In this sense, the very presence of the divine glory in human flesh,
gleaming from the eschatological mountain, represents the accomplish-
ment of human renewal. The flesh that is already formed by God is now
transformed to image the divine being, precisely in and through the incarnation of the Word. The purpose of the incarnation, which is integral to a
theological understanding of the transfiguration, is that human beings
may come to share the divine nature, as God has shared human nature.
The transfiguration thus symbolizes the salvific and eschatological purpose of the incarnation, revealing the human Jesus in his identity as the
divine Son. In the words of the Patristic maxim: 'He became what we are
that we might become what he is';[33] God becomes human that human
beings may become divine.[34]

An essential aspect of the transformation of believers, moreover, is that
transfiguration cannot be confined to so-called 'spiritual' realities. The
body is not incidental in a theology that embraces incarnation and
transfiguration. On the contrary, the body also shares in the hope of
redemption, just as Jesus' human body, shining with divine glory, remains
palpable. Being suffused with light, the body reveals its sacramental
capacity – and highest destiny – in disclosing the light and love of God. The

salvation into which the transfiguration draws the three disciples is as much physical as spiritual, as embracing of the body as of the soul and spirit. As the point of connection between heaven and earth, the incarnate Son entices human beings into his glory, a divine glory manifest in and through his flesh. Jesus' body is clothed in the garments of light, revealing not just his own identity but ours, not just the destiny of the soul but also the body.

This metamorphosis, moreover, is not only for human beings but extends to the whole creation. The sheer materiality of the incarnation, and the translucence of Jesus' body on the mount of transfiguration, ensures that nature itself is caught up in the deification of human beings: 'the entire cosmos will some day partake in the fruit of the incarnate'.[35] Just as human beings become translucent before the sight of the transfigured Christ, so creation will share in the divine light, participating in the effects of the transfiguration. The imagery of the mountain, and Peter's suggestion of constructing leafy tents, take the transfiguration in an ecological direction, embracing every aspect of the material world. In the end, the anthropology is both ecclesial and ecological, drawing the created world, as it is symbolized in the life of the Church – its sacraments, its prayer and its mission – into God's transfiguring future. There the lion will lie down with the lamb, human beings will cease their destruction, trees and rivers, valleys and hills, wild beasts and tame, forests and seas, will dwell in peace and flourish in fecundity and beauty. All creation, as the work of God's hands, will be gathered into the holy light on the mountain. The hope of salvation is the promise of a world re-made, all the diversity and complexity of creation enfolded in the one pure, uncontaminated beam of light. The transfiguration is about the renewing and restoring of the earth.

There is one final aspect that follows from the question of how the transfiguration works. The perception of the viewer (or reader) is central to an anthropological and, indeed, salvific understanding of the transfiguration. We have observed throughout this study that the transfiguration is improperly classified as a 'pronouncement story' – a story whose main point is a magisterial utterance by God or Jesus. Rather, the symbols of the transfiguration are as much concerned with the seeing as with the hearing; not just the words of the divine voice but the sight of the glory in Jesus' face. The incarnation indicates this change 'from a predominantly audible word that required the ear of obedience to a visible word'.[36] This is a vital point and one that words alone, with all their metaphorical and symbolic import, cannot sufficiently address. The role of the iconic, by means of the visual, needs also to be given a place.

Icons of the transfiguration, particularly in the Eastern tradition, enable the viewer to enter the world of the text in a different, though parallel, way. In general terms, icons are windows on the eternal, presentations of the heavenly world into which the viewer – that is, the worshipper – is drawn. For the supporters of icons in the debates of the eighth and ninth centuries, the incarnation not only permitted the making of icons – as against Old Testament prohibitions of graven images – but also made it necessary, since the invisible God was now rendered visible in the person of Jesus. The symbols which the icon portrays visually are the same symbols which the text articulates verbally. The icon makes it possible for the believer to see as well as hear, to grasp the vision of light as well as hearken to the voice proclaiming Jesus as the beloved Son, to be lifted by the Spirit into the light of God which the beauty of the text unveils.[37]

In the iconography of the transfiguration, the person of Christ – radiant and bright – is set within a mandorla, an oval or almond shape, and surrounded by a star, sometimes including three beams of light aimed at each of the prostrate disciples. The mandorla also stands for the cloud and the voice that issues from it. Often dark at its centre, signifying the darkness of God who remains transcendent and mysterious,[38] the mandorla signifies paradoxically both the light and the darkness of God, the accessibility yet absolute holiness of God beyond anything imaginable. The cloud is also associated symbolically with the Holy Spirit, so much so that, like the baptism, the revelation on the mountain takes on a trinitarian hue, disclosing the presence of Father, Son and Holy Spirit in and through the transfigured body of Jesus: 'This humanity revealed the divinity which is the splendour of the Three Persons.'[39] The luminous figure of Christ is the centre of the icon, as it is of the New Testament narratives, palpable and radiant, the whiteness flecked with gold. The brightness of his appearance symbolizes the uncreated light of God that illumines Jesus' flesh through the cloud of the Spirit. 'The disciples hear the Father, see the Son and are enveloped by the Holy Spirit.'[40]

If the mandorla is a way of depicting the revelation of a heavenly being, it follows that the meaning of the symbolism is perceptible only to the eyes of faith. A person of no faith eavesdropping on the event would fail to discern the radiance, including the presence of Moses and Elijah, and fail also to detect the voice.[41] The fact that the three disciples do see, even if they are confused and overcome, indicates that they possess a measure of faith, albeit partial. In the Synoptic accounts, they recognize the splendour and in 2 Peter are the designated eyewitnesses, perceiving with both the physical senses and those of faith (2 Pet. 1:16). The fourth evangelist has no hesitation in asserting that 'we beheld his glory' (John 1:14); later in John's Gospel, when the Father speaks from heaven, some of the crowd, who lack faith, mistake the sound for thunder (John 12:29). Faith is essential to see and hear aright. To perceive intuitively the symbols of the transfiguration is to recognize the theophany and be swept into the orbit of God's transforming future. The result is a deeper sharing in the divine nature: 'To see the divine light with bodily sight, as the disciples saw it on Mount Tabor, we must participate in and be transformed by it, according to our capacity.'[42]

At the same time, the faith itself and the ability to perceive are ultimately a divine gift. Sight and hearing – eyes and ears – are given from above so that, along with the revelation of God in the brightness of Jesus' flesh, comes the capacity to perceive it. Mark's Gospel makes this clear by setting the journey to Jerusalem, in which the transfiguration plays so crucial a part, within the context of the miraculous giving of sight to blind eyes (Mark 8:22–6; 10:45–52). On this journey, the disciples will fail to see and perceive, exposing their need for a miracle of faith. In 2 Peter, this miracle includes explicitly the capacity of the apostolic eyewitnesses to interpret the transfiguration aright and hand it on as part of the received body of faith. In the end, faith is not something we manufacture but is a gift of grace and love. The perceptive disciple sees and hears with eyes and ears that have been opened by the divine touch, and proclaims good news with a tongue set free from its chain (Mark 7:31–7). We perceive in line with our capacity to perceive, because 'seeing has many stages which lead from the outside to the inside';[43] but that ability is the creative gift and work of the Spirit.

These dimensions are visible for the believing community above all in the sacraments, where the Word is proclaimed and made tangible in earthly gifts of bread, wine, and water. The transfiguration becomes enfleshed anew in the eucharist which functions both as the epiphany of Christ's glory and as a foretaste of the heavenly banquet. The eucharist itself is profoundly transformative. It is no coincidence that the Eastern celebration of the eucharist uses the explicit language of metamorphosis for the changing of the elements, through the Holy Spirit, into the body and blood of Christ. Narrative, icon and symbol join together in the sacrament in uniting the believer to the glory of the mountain, in all its luminosity and beauty, bringing together in the most palpable way the incarnation, transfiguration, death, resurrection and parousia of Christ. The implications of the story of the transfiguration for worship and especially the eucharist are considerable. The transfiguration needs to be restored to its rightful place at the heart of Christian theology, if we are to regain its beauty in the life and worship of the Church.

The reciting of Jesus' transfiguration in light on the holy mountain, whether in narrative or iconic form, makes possible our transfiguration: formed in the likeness of Christ, from glory to glory. The three symbolic stages of the transfiguration narrative – ascent (*anabasis*), theophany, descent (*katabasis*) – are replayed in our experience.[44] Christ's ascent up the mountain is the symbolic prototype of our spiritual ascent to God,[45] just as his descent to face the cross is our calling, like Peter, to 'endure your share of pain and hard toil'.[46] Yet the journey of deification does not end until the resurrection, when the body as well as the soul participates in the full reality of the transfiguration (cf. 1 Cor. 15:35–49).[47] The Church embodies this transformation, as the community of those whose eucharistic life fills them with the divine light of transfiguration on the mountain.

The transfiguration, with all its symbolic wealth, is a vitally important story in the New Testament, standing at the heart of Christian faith. Its pervasive presence in the Gospels and elsewhere, as well as its theological significance, gives it a central place in the faith and worship of the Church. It is not simply one event among many in Jesus' ministry. On the contrary, it has a function that goes beyond any single episode in the life of Jesus, holding together things that are too often held apart. On the mount of transfiguration

we perceive that the living and the dead are one in Christ, that the old covenant and the new are inseparable, that the cross and the glory are of one, that the age to come is already here, that our human nature has a destiny in glory, that in Christ the final word is uttered and in Him alone the Father is well pleased.[48]

The symbols of the transfiguration cross the divide, bringing together the apocalyptic and the epiphanic, spirit and matter, divinity and humanity, glory and suffering, beauty and terror, present and future, the old age and the new, human beings and creation, and also, by extension, men and women. Greatest of all divisions, the transfiguration – like the incarnation on which it is based – crosses the otherwise impassable gulf between

Creator and creation. The transfiguration points back to the incarnation of the divine Word and forward to the resurrection and parousia. Through the enlivening presence of the Spirit, the revelation on the holy mountain unfolds the divinity and humanity of God before our eyes, in light and beauty, giving eschatological form to our own humanity and divinity in Christ.

Notes

1 This view is not new – the early Church came to speak of the fourfold use of Scripture, encompassing the corporate, individual, theological and moral dimensions of the text.

2 See Tillich, P., *Systematic Theology: Reason and Revelation, Being and God*, vol. 1, SCM, London, 1951, 239–41; also Lee, D., *Flesh and Glory: Symbol, Gender and Theology in the Gospel of John*, Crossroad, New York, 2002, 14–22.

3 It is possible to argue that the three disciples, after the transfiguration, could never have abandoned Jesus in the passion; yet human beings do forget in situations of crisis, especially when confronted by suffering they do not understand.

4 Von Balthasar, H. U., *The Glory of the Lord: A Theological Aesthetics*, vol. 7: *Theology: The New Covenant* (trans. B. McNeil, ed. J. Riches), T. & T. Clark, Edinburgh, 1989, 347.

5 See McGuckin, J. A., *The Transfiguration of Christ in Scripture and Tradition*, Edwin Mellen, Lewiston, NY, 1986, 109–13. While theophany is the main category of Orthodox interpretation, the eschatological dimension is also integral to its meaning in the East.

6 Ramsay, M., *The Glory of God and the Transfiguration of Christ*, 2nd edn, Darton, Longman & Todd, London, 1967, 137.

7 See Lee, *Flesh and Glory*, 48–50.

8 While Eastern theology argues that the being of God in the incarnation undergoes no change, the Western tradition is more open to such a notion, Roman Catholics tending to emphasize the incarnation itself and Protestants the cross as the locus of change in the being and self-manifestation of God.

9 Luz, U., *Matthew 8–20: A Commentary* (trans. J. E. Crouch, ed. H. Koester), Fortress, Minneapolis, MN, 2001, 400–2.

10 In this theological framework, the light is associated with divine energies (or powers) rather than essence, a view that does not sit easily

with Western theological thought; see Lossky, V., *The Mystical Theology of the Eastern Church*, James Clarke & Co., London, 1957, 67–90, 222–4.

11 Ouspensky, L. and Lossky, V., *The Meaning of Icons* (trans. G. E. H. Palmer and E. Kadloubovsky), St Vladimir's Seminary Press, New York, 1989, 211.

12 Lossky, *op. cit.*, 221.

13 Gregory Palamas, *The Triads* II.iii.20, in Nes, S., *The Uncreated Light: An Iconographical Study of the Transfiguration in the Eastern Church*, Eastern Christian Publications, Fairfax, VA, 2002, 122.

14 Von Balthasar, *Glory of the Lord*, vol. 7, 278.

15 Andrew of Crete, *Oratio* 7.4, in McGuckin, *op. cit.*, 201.

16 Barth, K., *Church Dogmatics: The Doctrine of God* (trans. R. H. L. Parker et al.), vol. II.1, T. & T. Clark, Edinburgh, 1957, 651–2, takes issue with a hostile Puritan stance, incorporating beauty into his own exposition of the doctrine of God.

17 Von Balthasar, H.U., *The Glory of the Lord: A Theological Aesthetics*, vol. 1: *Seeing the Form* (trans. E. Leiva-Merikakis, ed. J. Fessio and J. Riches), Ignatius Press, San Francisco, 1982, 19–20, 118–19.

18 See Barth, *op. cit.*, 651–6.

19 *Ibid.*, 665.

20 Von Balthasar, *Glory of the Lord*, vol. 7, 293.

21 Von Balthasar, *Glory of the Lord*, vol. 1, 32–3.

22 Dionysius the Areopagite, *The Divine Names* IV.13, quoted in *ibid.*, 122.

23 Von Balthasar, *Glory of the Lord*, vol. 7, 389.

24 See von Balthasar, *Glory of the Lord*, vol. 1, 18, who observes that beauty 'dances as an uncontained splendour around the double constellation of the true and the good and their inseparable relation to one another'.

25 Von Balthasar, *Glory of the Lord*, vol. 7, 315–16.

26 Nes, *op. cit.*, 73.

27 Feminist theologians speak of this as a kind of reading 'against the grain', although strictly the 'grain' of the symbolism is open, by definition, to more inclusive readings. On the flesh of Jesus as representative, see Lee, *Flesh and Glory*, pp.52–64.

28 The Feast of the Transfiguration probably goes back to the fourth century. Since the eighth century it has been a major feast in the East. In the West, it was made a formal feast in the fifteenth century but one of secondary importance. See Ouspensky and Lossky, 211.

29 Peter Steele, Poem 68, *Potomac*, quoted in Rayment, C., *The Shapes of Glory: The Writings of Peter Steele*, Spectrum Publications, Adelaide, 2000, 149.

30 Tolkien, J. R. R., 'On Fairy Stories', in Tolkien, J. R. R., *Tree and Leaf*, Unwin Books, London, 1964, 60–1.

31 Nes, *op. cit.*, 29.

32 See Jerome, *Commentary on Matthew* 3.17.2, in McGuckin, *op. cit.*, 270–1.

33 Athanasius, *On the Incarnation* 54, in *ibid.*, 119.

34 Nes, *op. cit.*, 30–2.

35 *Ibid.*, 75.

36 Von Balthasar, *Glory of the Lord*, vol. 7, 273–4.

37 This way of reading the transfiguration is associated particularly with Hesychasm (from the Greek meaning 'silence') and the fourteenth-century mystical theologian, Gregory Palamas.

38 Easter theology moves from the *kataphatic* dimension (what can be said about God) to the *apophatic* (what is beyond words), both being necessary for theology; see Nes, *op. cit.*, 39–42.

39 Lossky, *op. cit.*, 149.

40 McGuckin, *op. cit.*, 106–9, and Nes, *op. cit.*, 47. For a prayerful meditation on the transfiguration icon, see especially Williams, R., The Transfiguration, in *The Dwelling of the Light: Praying with Icons of Christ*, John Garratt Publishing, Melbourne, 2003, 1–19.

41 This view gives a rather different slant on the debate over whether the transfiguration has an historical basis.

42 Lossky, *op. cit.*, 224.

43 Von Balthasar, *Glory of the Lord*, vol. 7, 288.

44 Nes, *op. cit.*, 1–2.

45 Andrew of Crete, *Oratio* 7.1, in McGuckin, *op. cit.*, 200–1; see Luz, *op. cit.*, 401.

46 Augustine, *Homily* 28.6, in McGuckin, *op. cit.*, 277.

47 Nes, *op. cit.*, 63. Gregory Palamas and the Hesychasts were criticized for their conviction that the body participated in the divine nature (on account of the incarnation).

48 Ramsay, *op. cit.*, 144.

References and Bibliography

Allison, D. C., *The New Moses: A Matthean Typology*, Fortress, Minneapolis, MN, 1993.

Ashton, J., *Understanding the Fourth Gospel*, Clarendon, Oxford, 1990.

Balthasar, H. U. von, *The Glory of the Lord: A Theological Aesthetics*, vol. 1: *Seeing the Form* (trans. E. Leiva-Merikakis, ed. J. Fessiono and J. Riches), Ignatius Press, San Fransisco, 1982.
— *The Glory of the Lord: A Theological Aesthetics*, vol. 7: *Theology: The New Covenant* (trans. B McNeil, ed. J Riches) T. and T. Clark, Edinburgh, 1989.

Barr, J., 'Abba Isn't Daddy', *Journal of Theological Studies* 39, 1988, 28–47.

Barrett, C. K., *A Commentary on the Second Epistle to the Corinthians*, A. & C. Black, London, 1973.
— *The Gospel According to St. John: An Introduction with Commentary and Notes on the Greek Text*, 2nd edn, SPCK, London, 1978.

Barth, K., *Church Dogmatics: The Doctrine of God* (trans. R. H. L. Parker *et al.*), vol. II.1, T. & T. Clark, Edinburgh, 1957.

Barton, S. C., *The Spirituality of the Gospels*, SPCK, London, 1992.
— 'The Transfiguration of Christ According to Mark and Matthew: Christology and Anthropology', in Avemarie, F. and Lichtenberger, H. (eds), *Auferstehung – Resurrection*, J. C. B. Mohr (Paul Siebeck), Tübingen, 2001, 231–46.

Bauckham, R., *Jude, 2 Peter*, Word Books, Waco, TX, 1986.
— *The Climax of Prophecy: Studies on the Book of Revelation*, T. & T. Clark, Edinburgh, 1993.

Beale, G. K., *The Book of Revelation: A Commentary on the Greek Text*, Eerdmans, Grand Rapids, MI, 1999.

Beare, F. W., *The Gospel According to Matthew*, Blackwell, Oxford, 1981.

Beasley-Murray, G. R., *John*, Word Books, Waco, TX, 1987.

Behm, J., 'Morphê, Morphoô, Morphôsis, Metamorphoô', in Kittel, G. (ed.), *Theological Dictionary of the New Testament*, vol. 4, Eerdmans, Grand Rapids, MI, 1967, 742–59.

Best, E., 'The Markan Redaction of the Transfiguration', in Livingstone, E. A. (ed.), *International Congress on Biblical Studies*, Akademie, Berlin, 1982, 41–53.

Boobyer, G. H., *St. Mark and the Transfiguration Story*, T. & T. Clark, Edinburgh, 1942.

Boring, M. E., 'Matthew', in *The New Interpreter's Bible*, Abingdon, Nashville, TN, 1995, 8, 361–7.

Bornkamm, G., 'The Stilling of the Storm in Matthew', in Bornkamm, G., Barth, G. and Held, H. J. (eds), *Traditional Interpretation in Matthew*, SCM, London, 1963, 52–7.

Brouwer, W., *The Literary Development of John 13–17: A Chiastic Reading*, Society of Biblical Literature, Atlanta, GA, 2000.

Brower, K., 'Mark 9:1: Seeing the Kingdom in Power', *Journal for the Study of the New Testament* 6, 1980, 17–41.

Brown, R. E., *The Gospel According to John*, 2 vols, Doubleday, New York, 1966.
— *The Death of the Messiah – From Gethsemane to the Grave: A Commentary on the Passion Narratives in the Four Gospels*, 2 vols, Doubleday, New York, 1994.

Brown, R. E. et al., 'The Mother of Jesus in the Gospel of John', in *Mary in the New Testament: A Collaborative Assessment by Protestant and Roman Catholic Scholars*, Fortress, Philadelphia, 1978, 179–218.

Bultmann, R., *The History of the Synoptic Tradition* (trans. J. Marsh), Blackwell, Oxford, 1963.
— *The Gospel of John* (trans. G. R. Beasley-Murray), Blackwell, Oxford, 1971.

Butter, P. (ed.), *The Complete Poems of Edwin Muir*, The Association for Scottish Literary studies, Aberdeen, 1991.

Byrne, B., *The Hospitality of God: A Reading of Luke's Gospel*, Liturgical Press, Collegeville, MN, 2000.

Caird, G. B., 'The Transfiguration', *Expository Times* 67, 1955–56, 291–4.
— *Saint Luke*, Penguin Books, Harmondsworth, 1963.

Chilton, B. D., 'The Transfiguration: Dominical Assurance and Apostolic Vision', *New Testament Studies* 27, 1981, 115–24.

Craddock, F. B., *Luke*, John Knox, Louisville, KY, 1990.

Cranfield, C. E. B., *The Gospel According to Saint Mark: An Introduction and Commentary*, Cambridge University Press, Cambridge, 1959.

Crump, D., *Jesus the Intercessor: Prayer and Christology in Luke–Acts*, J. C. B. Mohr (Paul Siebeck), Tübingen, 1992.

Danker, E. W., '2 Peter', in Krodel, G. (ed.), *The General Letters: Hebrews, James, 1–2 Peter, Jude, 1–2–3 John*, Fortress, Minneapolis, MN, 1995, 84–93.

Davies, W. D. and Allison, D. C., *A Critical and Exegetical Commentary on the Gospel According to Saint Matthew*, 3 vols (ed. J. A. Emerton et al.), T. & T. Clark, Edinburgh, 1988–97.

Doble, P., *The Paradox of Salvation: Luke's Theology of the Cross*, Cambridge University Press, Cambridge, 1996.

Dodd, C. H., *The Interpretation of the Fourth Gospel*, Cambridge University Press, Cambridge, 1953.
— 'The Appearances of the Risen Christ: An Essay in Form-Criticism of the Gospels', in Nineham, D. E. (ed.), *Studies in the Gospels: Essays in Memory of R. H. Lightfoot*, Blackwell, Oxford, 1957, 9–35.

Donaldson, T. L., *Jesus on the Mountain: A Study in Matthean Theology*, JSOT Press, Sheffield, 1985.

Evans, C. A., *Mark* 8:27–16:20, vol. 34B (ed. R. P. Martin), Thomas Nelson, Nashville, TN, 2001.

Fitzmyer, J. A., *The Gospel According to Luke*, 2 vols, Doubleday, Garden City, NY, 1981, 1985.
— 'The Letter to the Romans', in Brown, R. E. et al. (eds), *The New Jerome Biblical Commentary*, Geoffrey Chapman, London, 1990, 830–68.

Fletcher-Louis, C. H. T., 'The Revelation of the Sacral Son of Man: The Genre, History of Religions Context and the Meaning of the Transfiguration', in Avemarie, F. and Lichtenberger, H. (eds),

Auferstehung – Resurrection, J. C. B. Mohr (Paul Siebeck), Tübingen, 2001, 247–98.

Foerster, W., '*Astrapê*', in Kittel, G. (ed.), *Theological Dictionary of the New Testament*, vol.1, Eerdmans, Grand Rapids, MI, 1964, 505.

Ford, J. M., *Redeemer, Friend and Mother: Salvation in Antiquity and in John*, Fortress, Minneapolis, MN, 1997.

Fossum, J. E., 'Ascensio, Metamorphosis: The "Transfiguration" of Jesus in the Synoptic Gospels', in Fossum, J. E., *The Image of the Invisible God: Essays on the Influence of Jewish Mysticism on Early Christology* (N. T. O. A. 30), Vandenhoeck & Ruprecht, Göttingen, 1995, 71–94.

Furnish, P. V., *II Corinthians: A New Translation with Introduction and Commentary*, Doubleday, New York, 1984.

Gregory, 'On the Holy Passover Xl.v.633–636', in Migne, J.-P. (ed.), *Patrologia Graeca*, 36.

Gundry, R. H., *Matthew: A Commentary on His Handbook for a Mixed Church under Persecution*, 2nd edn, Eerdmans, Grand Rapids, MI, 1994.

Hagner, D. A., *Matthew 14–28*, vol. 2, Word Books, Dallas, TX, 1995.

Harrington, D. J., *The Gospel of Matthew*, Liturgical Press, Collegeville, MN, 1991.
— 'Jude and 2 Peter', in Senior, D. P. and Harrington, D. J. (eds), *1 Peter, Jude and 2 Peter*, Liturgical Press, Collegeville, MN, 2003, 159–299.

Harrington, W. J., *Luke, Gracious Theologian: The Jesus of Luke*, Columba Press, Dublin, 1997.

Heil, J. P., *The Transfiguration of Jesus: Narrative Meaning and Function of Mark 9:2–8, Matt 17:1–8 and Luke 9:28–36*, Editrice Pontificio Istituto Biblico, Rome, 2000.

Hooker, M. D., '"What Doest Thou Here, Elijah?": A Look at St. Mark's Account of the Transfiguration', in Hurst, L. D. and Wright, N. T. (eds), *The Glory of Christ in the New Testament*, Clarendon, Oxford, 1987, 59–70.
— *The Gospel According to St. Mark*, A. & C. Black, London, 1991.

Iersel, B. M. F. van, *Mark: A Reader-Response Commentary*, Sheffield Academic Press, Sheffield, 1998.

Jackson, H. M., 'The Death of Jesus in Mark and the Miracle from the Cross', *New Testament Studies* 33, 1987, 16–37.

Johnson, L. T., *The Gospel of Luke*, Liturgical Press, Collegeville, MN, 1991.

Juel, D. H., *Mark*, Augsburg, Minneapolis, MN, 1990.

Kee, H. C., 'The Transfiguration in Mark: Epiphany or Apocalyptic Vision', in Reumann, J. (ed.), *Understanding the Sacred Text: Essays in Honor of Morton S. Enslin on the Hebrew Bible and Christian Beginnings*, Judson Press, Valley Forge, PA, 1972, 135–52.

Kelly, J. N. D., *A Commentary on the Epistles of Peter and of Jude* (ed. H. Chadwick), A. & C. Black, London, 1969.

Kenny, A., 'The Transfiguration and the Agony in the Garden', *Catholic Biblical Quarterly* 19, 1957, 444–52.

Kingsbury, J. D., *Matthew: Structure, Christology, Kingdom*, Fortress, Philadelphia, 1975.
— *Conflict in Luke: Jesus, Authorities, Disciples*, Fortress, Minneapolis, MN, 1991.

Kittel, G. and Rad, G. von, '*Doxa*', in Kittel, G. (ed.), *Theological Dictionary of the New Testament*, vol. 2, Eerdmans, Grand Rapids, MI, 1964, 233–53.

Kooy, V. H., 'The Transfiguration Motif in the Gospel of John', in Cook, J. I. (ed.), *Saved by Hope*, Eerdmans, Grand Rapids, MI, 1978, 64–78.

Lee, D., *The Symbolic Narratives of the Fourth Gospel: The Interplay of Form and Meaning*, Sheffield Academic Press, Sheffield, 1994.
—*Flesh and Glory: Symbol, Gender and Theology in the Gospel of John*, Crossroad, New York, 2002.
—'Transfiguration and the Gospel of John', in Kendall, D. and O'Collins, G. (eds), *In Many and Diverse Ways: A Festschrift Honoring Jacques Dupuis*, Orbis, Maryknoll, NY, 2003, 158–69.

Liefeld, W. L., 'Transfigure, Transfiguration, Transform', in Brown, C. (ed.), *The New International Dictionary of New Testament Theology*, vol. 3, 861–4.

Lightfoot, R. H., *The Gospel Message of St. Mark*, Clarendon, Oxford.

Lossky, V., *The Mystical Theology of the Eastern Church*, James Clarke & Co., London, 1957.

Luz, U., *Matthew 8–20: A Commentary* (trans. J. E. Crouch, ed. H. Koester), Fortress, Minneapolis, MN, 2001.

Magness, J. L., *Sense and Absence: Structure and Suspension in the Ending of Mark's Gospel*, Scholars Press, Atlanta, GA, 1986.

Malina, B. J., *The New Testament World: Insights from Cultural Anthropology*, SCM, London, 1981.

Marcus, J., *The Way of the Lord: Christological Exegesis of the Old Testament in the Gospel of Mark*, Westminster/John Knox, Louisville, KY, 1992.

Marshall, I. H., *The Gospel of Luke*, Eerdmans, Grand Rapids, MI, 1978.

Martin, R. P., 'The Theology of Jude, 1 Peter and 2 Peter', in Martin, R. P. and Chester, A. (eds), *The Theology of the Letters of James, Peter, and Jude*, Cambridge University Press, Cambridge, 1994, 63–163.

Mauser, U., *Christ in the Wilderness: The Wilderness Theme in the Second Gospel and its Basis in the Biblical Tradition*, SCM, London, 1963.

McCurley, F. R., '"and after Six Days" (Mark 9:2): A Semitic Literary Device', *Journal of Biblical Literature* 93, 1974, 67–81.

McGuckin, J. A., *The Transfiguration of Christ in Scripture and Tradition*, Edwin Mellen, Lewiston, NY, 1986.

Metzger, B. M., *A Textual Commentary on the Greek New Testament*, 2nd edn, United Bible Societies, London, 1975.

Michaelis, W., '*Eisodos, Exodos, Diexodos*', in Kittel, G. (ed.), *Theological Dictionary of the New Testament*, vol. 5, Eerdmans, Grand Rapids, MI, 1967a, 103–9.
— '*Horama*', in Kittel, G. (ed.), *Theological Dictionary of the New Testament*, vol. 5, Eerdmans, Grand Rapids, MI, 1967b, 371–2.

Miller, R. D., 'Historicizing the Trans-Historical: The Transfiguration Narrative (Mark 9:2–8, Matt 17:1–8, Luke 9:28–36)', *Forum* 10, 1994, 219–48.
— 'Is There Independent Attestation for the Transfiguration in 2 Peter?' *New Testament Studies* 50, 1996, 620–5.

— 'Source Criticism and the Limits of Certainty: The Lukan Transfiguration Story as a Test Case', *ETL* 74, 1998, 127–44.

Moloney, F. J., *Signs and Shadows: Reading John 5–12*, Fortress, Minneapolis, MN, 1996.
— *The Gospel of John*, Liturgical Press, Collegeville, MN, 1998.
— *The Gospel of Mark: A Commentary*, Hendrickson, Peabody, MA, 2002.

Morris, L., *Luke*, 2nd edn, InterVarsity Press, Leicester, 1988.

Moses, A. D. A., *Matthew's Transfiguration Story and Jewish–Christian Controversy* (ed. S. E. Porter), Sheffield Academic Press, Sheffield, 1996.

Murphy-O'Connor, J., 'What Really Happened at the Transfiguration?', *Bible Review* 3, 1987, 8–21.
— 'The Second Letter to the Corinthians', in Brown, R. E. et al. (eds), *The New Jerome Biblical Commentary*, Geoffrey Chapman, London, 1990, 816–29.

Myers, C., *Binding the Strong Man: A Political Reading of Mark's Story of Jesus*, Orbis, Maryknoll, NY, 1990.

Neirynck, F., 'Minor Agreements Matthew–Luke in the Transfiguration Story', in Hoffmann, P. (ed.), *Orientierung an Jesus: Zur Theologie der Synoptiker*, Herder, Freiburg, 1973, 253–65.

Nes, S., *The Uncreated Light: An Iconographical Study of the Transfiguration in the Eastern Church*, Eastern Christian Publications, Fairfax, VA, 2002.

Neyrey, J., *2 Peter, Jude: A New Translation with Introduction and Commentary* AB 37c, Doubleday, New York, 1993.

Nineham, D. E., *Saint Mark*, Penguin Books, Harmondsworth, 1963.

Nolland, J., *Luke 1–9:20*, vol. 1, Word Books, Dallas, TX, 1989.
— *Luke 9:21–18:34*, vol. 2 , Word Books, Dallas, TX, 1993.

O'Collins, G., *The Easter Jesus*, Darton, Longman & Todd, London, 1973.

Oepke, A., *'Nephelê'*, in Kittel, G. (ed.), *Theological Dictionary of the New Testament*, vol. 4, Eerdmans, Grand Rapids, MI, 1967, 902–10.

Öhler, M., 'Die Verklärung (Mk 9:1–8): Die Ankunft der Herrschaft Gottes auf der Erde', *Novum Testamentum* 38, 1996, 197–217.

Ouspensky, L. and Lossky, V., *The Meaning of Icons* (trans. G. E. H. Palmer and E. Kadloubovsky), St Vladimir's Seminary Press, New York, 1989.

Pamment, M., 'Moses and Elijah in the Story of the Transfiguration', *Expository Times* 92, 1981, 338–9.

Patte, D., *The Gospel According to Matthew: A Structural Commentary on Matthew's Faith*, Fortress, Philadelphia, 1987.

Perkins, P., 'The Gospel According to John', in Brown, R. E. et al. (eds), *The New Jerome Biblical Commentary*, Geoffrey Chapman, London, 1990, 942–85.
— *First and Second Peter, James, and Jude*, John Knox, Louisville, KY, 1995.

Perry, J. M., *Exploring the Transfiguration Story*, Sheed & Ward, Kansas City, MO, 1993.

Philo, *The Life of Moses* (trans. F. H. Colson) (Loeb Classical Library, vol. 6 of 12), Harvard University Press, Cambridge, MA, 1984.
— *Questions and Answers on Genesis* (trans. R. Marcus) (Loeb Classical Library, vol. Supplement I of 12), Harvard University Press, Cambridge, MA, 1979.
— *Questions and Answers on Exodus* (trans. R. Marcus) (vol. Supplement II of 12), Harvard University Press, Cambridge, MA, 1987.

Plummer, A. et al. (eds), *A Critical and Exegetical Commentary on the Second Epistle of St. Paul to the Corinthians*, T. & T. Clark, Edinburgh, 1915.
— *A Critical and Exegetical Commentary on the Gospel According to St. Luke*, 5th edn, T. & T. Clark, Edinburgh, 1922.

Potteriede I. de la , 'L'emploi de eis dans Saint Jean et ses incidences théologiques', *Biblica* 43, 1962, 366–87.

Ramsay, M., *The Glory of God and the Transfiguration of Christ*, 2nd edn, Darton, Longman & Todd, London, 1967.

Rayment, C., *The Shapes of Glory: The Writings of Peter Steele*, Spectrum Publications, Adelaide, 2000.

Reicke, B., *The Epistles of James, Peter, and Jude, Translated with an Introduction and Notes*, Doubleday, New York, 1964.

Reid, B., *The Transfiguration: A Source- and Redaction-Critical Study of Luke 9:28–36* (Cahiers de la Revue Biblique), J. Gabalda, Paris, 1993.

Riesenfeld, H., *Jésus transfiguré: l'arrière-plan du récit évangélique de la transfiguration de Notre-Seigneur*, Munksgaard, Copenhagen, 1947.

Ringe, S. H., 'Luke 9:28–36: The Beginning of an Exodus', *Semeia* 28, 1983, 83–99.
— *Luke*, Westminster/John Knox, Louisville, KY, 1995.

Schmidt, T. E., 'The Penetration of Barriers and the Revelation of Christ in the Gospels', *Novum Testamentum* 34, 1992, 229–46.

Schnackenburg, R., *The Gospel According to St. John*, 3 vols, Burns & Oates, London, 1968–82.

Schneiders, S. M., *Written That You May Believe: Encountering Jesus in the Fourth Gospel*, Crossroad, New York, 1999.

Schnelle, U., *Antidocetic Christology in the Gospel of John: An Investigation of the Place of the Fourth Gospel in the Johannine School* (trans. L. M. Maloney), Fortress, Minneapolis, MN, 1992.
— *Das Evangelium nach Johannes*, Evangelische Verlagsanstalt, Leipzig, 1998.

Schulz, S., *'Episkiaziô'*, in Kittel, G. and Friedrich, G. (eds), *Theological Dictionary of the New Testament*, vol. 7, Eerdmans, Grand Rapids, MI, 1971, 399–400.

Schweizer, E., *The Good News According to Mark: A Commentary on the Gospel* (trans. D. H. Madvig), SPCK, London, 1970.
— *Jesus*, SCM, London, 1971.
— *The Good News According to Matthew: A Commentary on the Gospel* (trans. D. E. Green), SPCK, London, 1975.
— *The Good News According to Luke* (trans. D. E. Green), SPCK, London, 1984.

Scott, M., *Sophia and the Johannine Jesus*, Sheffield Academic Press, Sheffield, 1992.

Senior, D., *The Passion of Jesus in the Gospel of Mark*, Michael Glazier, Wilmington, DE, 1984.
— *Matthew*, Abingdon, Nashville, TN, 1998.

Sim, D. C., *The Gospel of Matthew and Christian Judaism: The History and Social Setting of the Matthean Community* (ed. John Barclay et al.), T. & T. Clark, Edinburgh, 1998.

Smith, D. M., *Johannine Christianity: Essays on Its Setting, Sources, and Theology*, T. & T. Clark, Edinburgh, 1984.

Stegner, W. R., 'The Use of Scripture in Two Narratives of Early Jewish Christianity (Matth 4.1–11; Mark 9.2–8)', in Evans, C. A. and Sanders, J. A. (eds), *Early Christian Interpretation of the Scriptures of Israel: Investigations and Proposals*, Sheffield Academic Press, Sheffield, 1997, 111–12.

Stein, R. H., 'Is the Transfiguration (Mark 9:2–8) a Misplaced Resurrection Account?' *JBL* 95, 1976, 79–96.

Stock, A., *The Method and Message of Matthew*, Liturgical Press, Collegeville, MN, 1994.

Talbert, C. H., *Reading Luke: A Literary and Theological Commentary on the Third Gospel*, Crossroad, New York, 1982.

Tannehill, R. C., *Luke*, Abingdon, Nashville, TN, 1996.

Taylor, V., *The Gospel According to St. Mark*, Macmillan, London, 1952.

Templeton, D. A., *The New Testament as True Fiction: Literature, Literary Criticism, Aesthetics* (ed. G. Aichele), Sheffield Academic Press, Sheffield, 1999.

Thompson, M. M., *The Promise of the Father: Jesus and God in the New Testament*, Westminster/John Knox, Louisville, KY, 2000.
— *The God of the Gospel of John*, Eerdmans, Grand Rapids, MI, 2001.

Thrall, M. E., 'Elijah and Moses in Mark's Account of the Transfiguration', *NTS* 16, 1969–70, 305–17.

Tiede, L., *Luke*, Augsburg, Minneapolis, MN, 1988.

Tillich, P., *Systematic Theology: Reason and Revelation, Being and God*, vol. 1, SCM, London, 1951.

Tolkien, J. R. R., 'On Fairy Stories', in Tolkien, J. R. R., *Tree and Leaf*, Unwin Books, London, 1964, 11–70.

Trites, A. A., 'The Transfiguration in the Theology of Luke: Some Redactional Links', in Hurst, L. D. and Wright, N. T. (eds), *The Glory of Christ in the New Testament*, Clarendon, Oxford, 1987, 71–81.

Tuckett, C. M., *Luke*, Sheffield Academic Press, Sheffield, 1996.

Viviano, B. T., 'The Gospel According to Matthew', in Brown, R. E. et al. (eds), *The New Jerome Biblical Commentary*, Geoffrey Chapman, London, 1990, 630–74.

Ward, G., 'Bodies: The Displaced Body of Jesus Christ' in Millbank, J., Pickstock, C. and Ward, G. (eds), *Radical Orthodoxy*, Routledge, London.

Wenham, D., and Moses, A. D. A., '"There Are Some Standing Here … ": Did They Become the "Reputed Pillars" of the Jerusalem Church? Some Reflections on Mark 9:1, Galatians 2:9 and the Transfiguration', *Novum Testamentum* 36, 1994, 146–63.

Whitacre, R. A., *John*, InterVarsity Fellowship, Leicester, 1999.

Williams, R. *The Dwelling of the Light. Praying with Icons of Christ*, John Garratt Publishing, Melbourne, 2003.

Wink, W., 'Mark 9:2–8', *Interpretation* 36, 1982.

Wright, N. T., 'Reflected Glory: 2 Cor. 3:18' in Hurst L. D. and Wright, N. T. (eds) *The Glory of Christ in the New Testament: Studies in Christology in Memory of George Bradford Caird*, Clarendon, Oxford, 1987, 139–50.

Wybrew, H. *Orthodox Feasts of Jesus Christ and the Virgin Mary. Liturgical Texts with Commentary*, St. Vladimir's Seminary Press, New York, 2000.

Yee, G. A., *Jewish Feasts and the Gospel of John*, Michael Glazer, Wilmington, DE, 1989.

Ziesler, J. A., 'The Transfiguration Story and Markan Soteriology', *Expository Times* 81, 1970.

Index

Index of Names and Subjects